1978

School of Design Basel, Switzerland
Foundation Program

VAN NOSTRAND REINHOLD COMPANY
NEW YORK   CINCINNATI   TORONTO   LONDON   MELBOURNE

Manfred Maier

The Foundation Program at the School of Design
Basel, Switzerland

Basic Principles of Design

This book was originally published in Switzerland
under the title
Elementare Entwurfs- und Gestaltungsprozesse.
Die Grundkurse an der Kunstgewerbeschule
Basel, Schweiz.
by Verlag Paul Haupt Berne
Copyright © 1977 by Paul Haupt Berne
Conception and Design:
Manfred Maier
Photography:
Max Mathys
(Dimensional Design/Ruth Geshekter)
Cover Design:
Wolfgang Weingart
English version:
Joseph Finocchiaro
William Longhauser
Janet Longhauser

Library of Congress Catalog Card Number
77-3493
ISBN 0-442-24977-2 (v. 1)
ISBN 0-442-24978-0 (v. 2)
ISBN 0-442-24979-9 (v. 3)
ISBN 0-442-24980-2 (v. 4)

Printed in Switzerland

Composition: Schüler AG, Biel
Films: Aberegg-Steiner AG, Bern
Offset-Printing: Roto-Sadag SA, Geneva
Bookbinding: Roger Veihl, Geneva

Published in 1977 by
Van Nostrand Reinhold Company
A Division of Litton Educational Publishing, Inc.
450 West 33rd Street
New York, NY 10001, U.S.A.

Van Nostrand Reinhold Limited
1410 Birchmount Road
Scarborough, Ontario M1P 2E7, Canada

Van Nostrand Reinhold Australia Pty. Ltd.
17 Queen Street
Mitcham, Victoria 3132, Australia

Van Nostrand Reinhold Company Ltd.
Molly Millars Lane
Wokingham, Berkshire, England

16 15 14 13 12 11 10 9 8 7 6 5 4 3 2 1

Library of Congress Cataloging in Publication
Data

Maier, Manfred
Basic principles of design.
Translation of Elementare Entwurfs- und
Gestaltungsprozesse. Die Grundkurse an der
Kunstgewerbeschule Basel, Schweiz.
CONTENTS: v. 1. Object drawing, object and
museum drawing, nature drawing. — v. 2.
Memory drawing, technical drawing and per-
spective, lettering. — v. 3. Material studies,
textile design, color 2. — v. 4. Color 1, graphic
exercises, dimensional design.
1. Design—Study and teaching. I. Title
NK1170.M3413   745.4'07   77-3493
ISBN 0-442-24977-2 (v. 1)
ISBN 0-442-24978-0 (v. 2)
ISBN 0-442-24979-9 (v. 3)
ISBN 0-442-24980-2 (v. 4)

General Introduction

Kurt Hauert,
Head of the Foundation Program

The Foundation Program at the School of Design in Basel, Switzerland is a fundamental education in art and design. It offers a number of interrelated, equally important courses. Subjects include drawing, color, three-dimensional studies, materials and tools, and exercises in form, aesthetics, and concepts, all of which are designed to promote optical and tactical sensitivity, formal perception, manual dexterity, and a clear understanding of creative processes and to clarify the students' individual talents. The program enables them to choose future professional training in graphic design, photography, typography, display design, goldsmithery, pottery, fine art, sculpture, and other related fields.

To be admitted into the program, students must be at least 15 years old, pass an entrance examination, and attend all the classes. The one-year program includes 42 classroom hours per week. All classes are conducted at the school and are limited to a maximum of 24 students.

Most of the faculty members are also professionals in their field, certified specialists who are active in visual, creative areas. Throughout the entire program, the teachers are available for individual or group consultation, which ensures that every student has an equal opportunity for a successful training. The teaching-learning process varies with each course. It can progress in several directions: linear, from simple to difficult principles; punctual, a collection of experiences derived from individual assignments; or complex, an analysis of variation sequences as an insight into the creative process.

The current standards of the program are outlined in this series, and the working procedure is explained clearly and understandably in chronological sequence. In order to clarify the interrelationships among the courses, they are categorized according to the teaching-learning process involved. The entire visual-creative program is presented in four volumes, each of which is a complete unit in itself and provides an introduction, course descriptions, and detailed illustrations.

The Foundation Program is based on an objective, developmental educational system over the past thirty years. It disregards fashionable vogues but allows enough freedom to integrate necessary innovations. It offers a model for all teachers, students, and administrators who are interested in a critical, investigatory approach.

In conclusion special thanks are expressed to those who devoted their time and energy to the realization of this work.

5

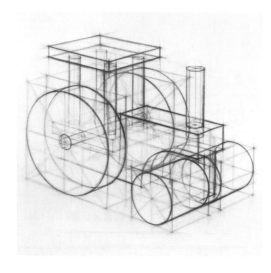

Table of Contents

Volume 1

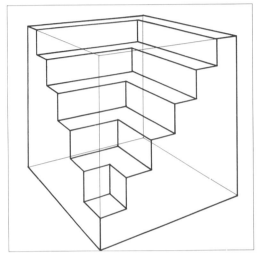
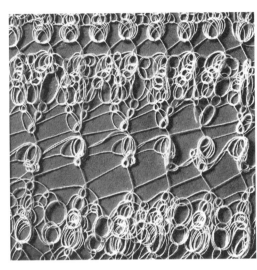

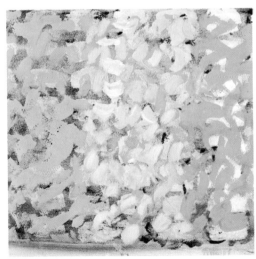
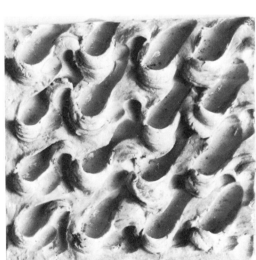

Volume 2

Volume 3

Volume 4

	Hours
Graphic Exercises	4
Color 2	3
Color 1	3
Object Drawing	4
Nature Drawing	2
Lettering	2
Memory Drawing	3
Textile Design	2
Dimensional Design	4
Literature, Language	2
Physical Education	2
Information	2
Technical Drawing and Perspective	3
Material Study	3
Object and Museum Drawing	3
	42

Number of faculty in the Foundation
Program   26
Number of students in the Foundation
Program in six parallel classes   130 ca.

Directorship:

until 1970 Emil Ruder
since 1971 Niklaus Morgenthaler
Head of the Foundation Program:
since 1971 Kurt Hauert

Faculty of the Foundation Program

Beck, A.	Economics	Bernoulli, L.	Architecture	1972–73
Biesele, I.	Graphic Design	Bühler, G.	Drawing	1968–69
Bollin, M.	Sculpture	Ganahl, K.	Press-editing	1966–67
Bürgin, G.	Decoration	Gruber, A.	Sculpture	1969–70
Burla, J.	Sculpture	Hartmann, H.	Drawing	1968–69
Eya, L.	Architecture	Hauert, K.	Drawing	1969–70
Gautschi, R.	Painting	Hernandez-Moor, L.	Textile Design	1972–73
Grossenbacher, M.	Sculpture	Keller, J.	Drawing	1974–75
Gürtler, A.	Letter Design	Lienhard, E.	Sculpture	1972–73
His, A.	Painting	Messerli, E.	Painting	1972–73
Hutter, J.	Painting	Ryser, F.	Painting	1973–74
Keller, T.	Painting	Stettler, G.	Painting	1967–68
Kern, R.	Painting	Stettler, P.	Painting	1974–75
Kern, U.	Drawing	Sulzbachner, M.	Painting	1968–69
Klotz, L.	Painting	Vollé, R.	Architecture	1968–69
Maier, M.	Graphic Design	Vieira, M.	Sculpture	1968–69
Mengelt, C.	Graphic Design	Weidmann, H.	Painting	1966–67
Mengelt, M.	Graphic Design			
Pola, P.	Painting			
Schäfer, E.	Drawing			
Sommer, H. P.	Graphic Design			
Thomann, M.	Language			
Tramèr, J.	Painting			
Von Tomei, J.	Graphic Design			
Zwimpfer, G.	Graphic Design			
Zwimpfer, M.	Graphic Design			

Volume | Memory Drawing
2 | Technical Drawing and Perspective
| Lettering

As in freehand drawing, the courses described in this volume are traditional media of western culture. They are very different in their content, appearance, and function. As means of communication they are based on the concepts: the representation of creative imagination and interpretation from the pictorial contents; the constructive, readable representation from mathematical discipline and the sequence of letter characters as a visual translation of language.

The purposes of the courses are to develop sensitivity to pictorial, spatial, and constructive imagination and to differentiate form, color value, composition, rhythm, and abstraction. Mastery of skills and techniques is achieved through continual investigation of the actual contents of the subject. As in freehand drawing, the teaching method is structured from simple to complex principles.

The elementary exercises in each subject are interrelated. Any uncertainty or lack of clarity is obvious at each phase of the investigation and can be recognized and corrected immediately under the guidance of the teacher. Comparative control of the student's work and critical evaluation of the working process expand the individual's consciousness and develop his faculty for independent judgement. The experience and knowledge derived from the individual exercises are prerequisites for further development. As in freehand drawing, the learning process involves continual linear differentiation.

Experience from the parallel taught subjects, color, freehand drawing, and perspective is applied in this course. In contrast to freehand-drawing courses, the students do not work from man-made or natural objects. The student learns to rely on his imagination and sensitivity. Creative ideas are derived from experience, and visual knowledge from memory and imagination. Ideas are abstracted into pictorial, dimensional representations.

In the elementary exercises themes supplied by the teacher are developed, scenes from daily life that everyone has seen or experienced: for example, table and chairs, geometric toys, breakfast, working table, or wash on the clothes-line. Representation of the human figure is deliberately avoided.

The goal is to achieve an interesting unity of composition. The following compositional questions and interrelations are investigated and clarified: volumetric appearance, division and depth of space, foreground-background relationship, overlapping, degree of perspective, kind and number of objects in a particular environment, grouping, contrast (light-dark, large-small, linear-surface), and formal elements (horizontal, vertical, diagonal, round).

In the first exercise a table and chairs or geometric toys are used as subjects. Many variations of each theme are sketched in pencil within a small format (10.5 × 14.8 cm). With the help of the teacher one of the sketches is chosen and enlarged (to 42 × 29.7 cm) in a freehand drawing. In the following exercises, a selected sketch serves as the formal foundation for color studies in tempera. Composition and color relationships are now considered. At first the number of colors is consciously limited to two pure colors, black, and white. Color variations are examined in gray-value studies in order to understand the light-dark effects of the composition. Colors can be mixed or changed for each sketch. One of the sketches is enlarged and refined. A further discipline involves remixing the colors: the effect of the same color is different because of the quantity change in the enlargement, and the spontaneity of the sketch is often lost. The color values in the sketch must be subtly translated in the enlargement. The results are discussed and compared in the classroom to expand the student's personal pictorial imagination. Creative experience from memory drawing is one of the preliminary steps toward illustration.

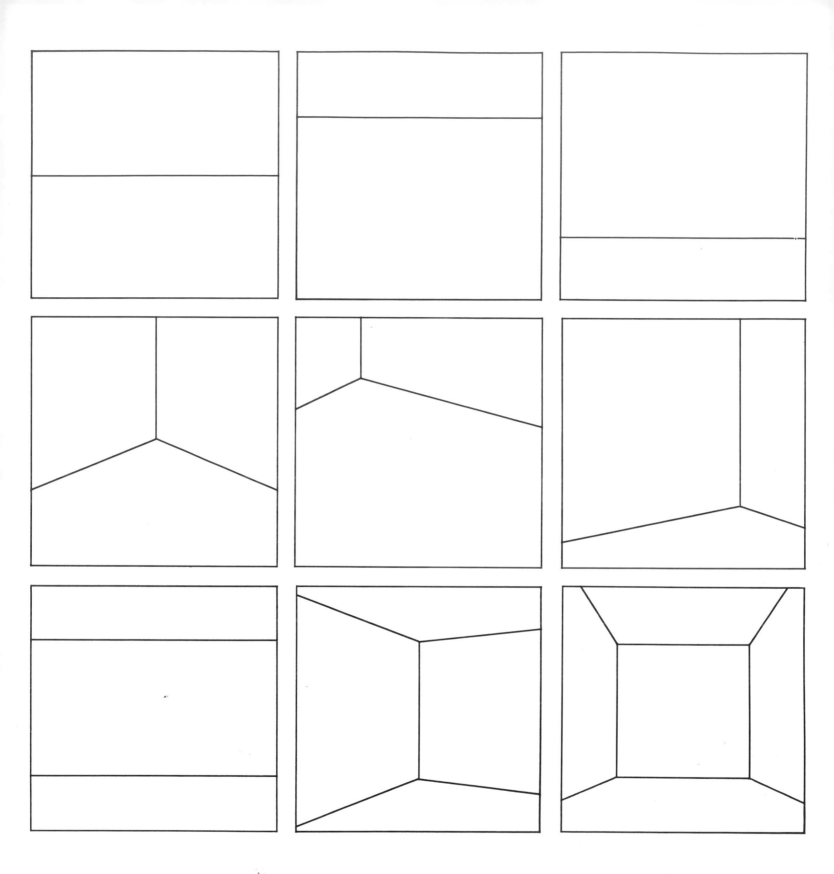

These examples serve as the basis for further sketches. They show how dimensional appearances can be represented by simple organization of the format.

The top row shows:
a wall and floor in the same relationship;
a small wall with a large floor surface;
and a large wall with a small floor.
The middle row shows:
two walls in the same relationship, a tabletop view of a volumetric corner developed with diagonals;
a large floor with a small wall;
and a large wall with a small floor.

The bottom row shows:
a ceiling-wall-floor arrangement;
an equal-sized ceiling and floor with a volumetric corner of different-size walls;
and a frontal view of a ceiling, floor, and three walls (central perspective).

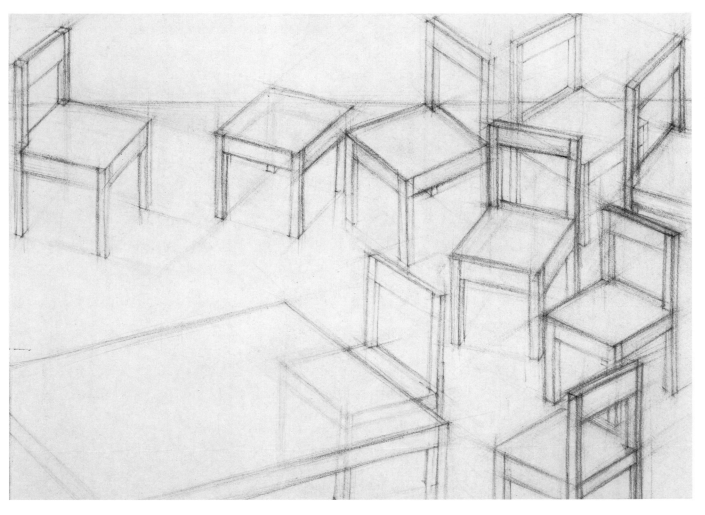

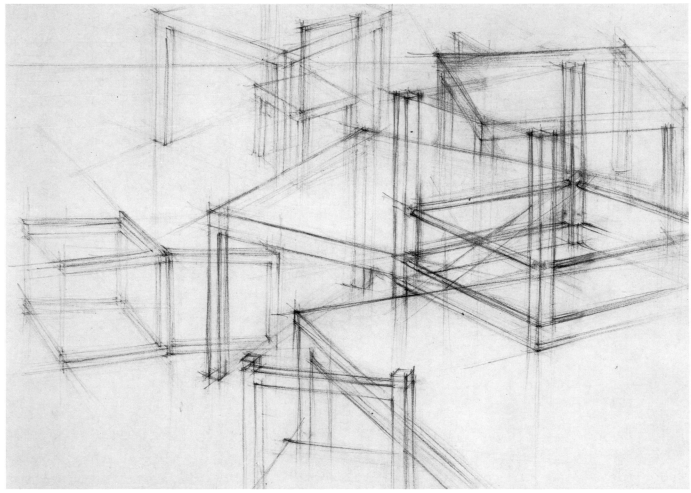

13

The illustrations here and on the preceding page show the work of different students on the theme table and chairs in space, executed in a large format. The three pencil drawings are carefully developed and differentiated in linear treatment, interpretation, and composition.

The example on the right was done by a student who had difficulties in sketching and developing a composition. It is produced with forms cut out of black paper, and, unlike the pencil drawings, the perspective is incorrect.

Gray-value studies and color sketches on the
theme breakfast, done in a smaller format, are
shown here. The number of colors in each sketch
is limited to two bright colors, black, and white.
The color study on the right was selected for
enlargement.

The enlargement of the sketch is shown here.
The colors used in the sketch should be remixed
as exactly as possible and transferred directly to
the enlargement. They often appear differently
in the final.

**Here and on the following ten pages a compari-
son of work on the same or on a similar theme
done by four different students demonstrates
the variation in personal imagination and interpretation.**

These photographs show the working area, the teacher, and students at work.

Gray-value studies and color sketches on the theme kitchen table are shown in a concentrated composition. Variations from light to dark are exceptionally clear, and each one gives a different feeling. The color study, below right, was selected for enlargement.

The enlargement of the sketch is shown here.

The students are sketching in pencil, working on color sketches, and making enlargements.

These three sketches on the theme breakfast were done directly with the brush, using black, white, and gray tones.

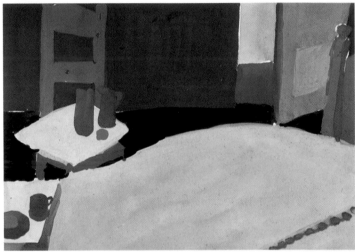

In these sketches on the same theme the differentiated treatment of the foreground and the checkered floor is particularly interesting. In this interpretation of the theme the desired wish appears to be breakfast served in bed.

Two bright colors, black, and white were used for this enlargement. Both color sketches were selected for enlargement because of the spontaneous working method and the partially glazed application of the paint.

Three gray-value studies and color sketches on the theme breakfast are shown here. The color sketches were executed in the same two colors; black, and white. The student developed a large number of possibilities by utilizing various mixing combinations. Individual objects advance or recede; the letterlike forms, numbers, and striped wallpaper are decorative elements.

The color sketch above was selected for the enlargement on the right.

The three photographs on the right show the working area, students at work, and the teacher suggesting a correction.

These compositional studies were done in pencil on the theme worktable. The sketch above center was selected for further investigation. In the illustration below, it is refined for enlargement and duplication.

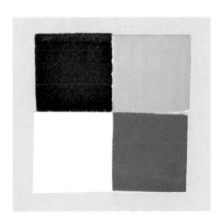

In the gray-value and color studies of the selected composition both bright colors were changed. The above unmixed-color combination was used in the enlargement. The corresponding sketch appears on the following page.

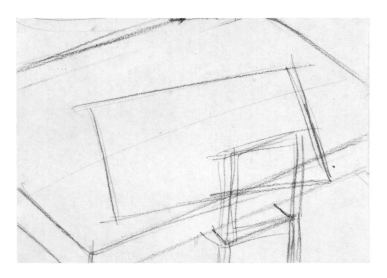

These pencil sketches on the theme worktable
show how the student begins with a clear idea
and tries to develop it. The composition below
right was selected as the basis for the color study.

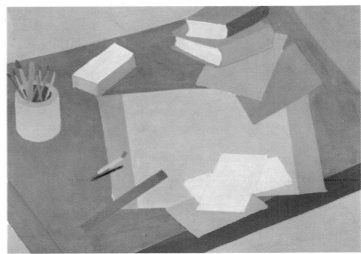

The use of white as a color in some of the color studies here and on the following pages is very interesting. Remaining light tones create a balance.

The enlargement of the adjacent color study is
shown here.

Mixtures of two bright colors, black, and white,
shown below left, form the palette for the color
studies and the resulting enlargement.

The differentiated pencil sketches on the theme
worktable are rhythmically drawn and composed.

These gray-value and color studies were done from the sketches on the opposite page. A different dimensional appearance and atmosphere are created in each study by painting the table surface light or dark and by changing both bright colors.

37

In the enlargement from the above color sketch the details are more differentiated.

This study on the theme schoolroom, achieved in a definite, spontaneous working method, was based on sketches.

On the following pages studies by three students on the theme wash on the clothesline clarify the different creative possibilities. The translation of the theme varies with personal experience and interpretation. The use of white as a color must be arranged harmoniously in a dark environment.

The first illustration shows wash hanging in the attic. The lightest color is blended with slightly darker tones and repeated in the lower-left corner.

In the second illustration towels hanging in the laundry room are represented with an open door leading outside. The light enters the room from outside without producing a harsh area that would disturb the entire composition.

The third illustration shows wash hanging between two apartment houses. Abundant repetition of light areas in different gradations and sizes produces a dynamic effect through the contrast of swirling and straight forms. The lines form an additional rhythmical element.

Many students have been introduced to geometry in secondary school. Plane geometry, a subdivision of the subject that includes simple, fundamental constructions as bisected angles, parallel projections, polygonal series, and the similarity ratio, forms the foundation for representational geometry. These fundamental constructions are applied in elementary exercises and supplemented with dimensional, graphic elements. The simple representation of a basic object is studied in parallel perspective. An understanding of the function of complicated constructions and the ability to draw them are developed through three-part axonometric, orthographic, and oblique projections. Students learn perspective and its principles through central projection in conjunction with photography. Extreme dimensional situations are consciously constructed and distorted beyond the normal field of vision; the difference is obvious between the perceived foreshortening in freehand drawing and the constructed perspective from a fixed viewpoint.

Drawing involving mathematical disciplines demands a neat representation, precision, and the concentration of the student. These skills are achieved through constant exercises with the appropriate tools and materials, especially ruling pen and compass. In professional practice they can be extended to production or architectural drawing, a technical specialty with recognized standards.

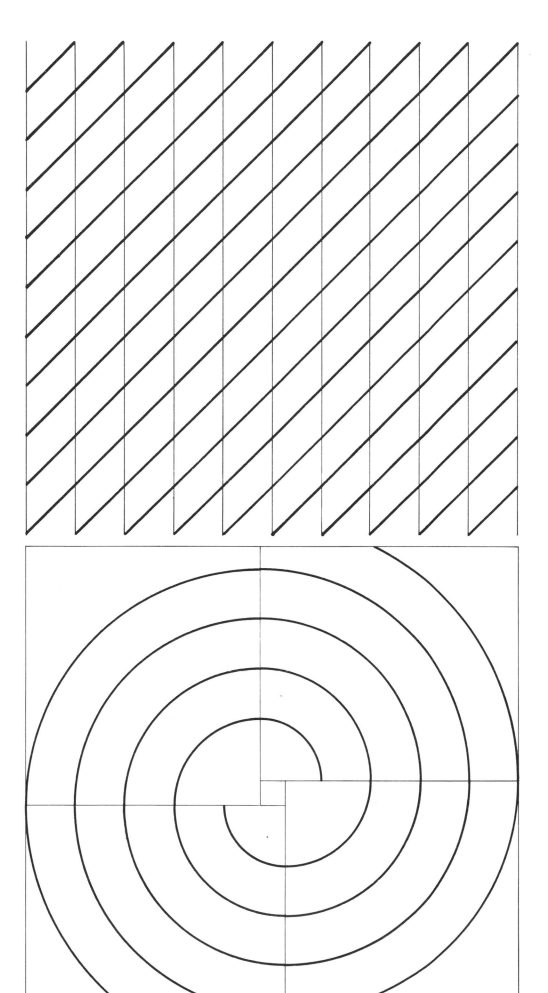

In the beginning of this course, simple prepara-
tory exercises explain correct handling of the
materials and tools. The students learn to use
T-square, triangle, pencil, ruling pen, compass,
ink, paper, and drawing board. At the beginning
they use pen-and-ink over pencil sketches: later
inking pens such as Rapidographs can be used.

On the left a preliminary study is shown.

The Archimedes spiral can be approximated by
constructing arches with their centers at the corners of polygons. With very small radii, the interior edge of the curve is deformed and needs
more than four radial points. These curves are
drawn directly in ink without preliminary pencil
sketches to avoid difficulties in tracing the curves
precisely.

Uses of the small, drop, and extension compasses are explained by the teacher, and the students experiment with them on sketch paper. Compass exercises include the construction of central-axis circles, with the constant reduction or enlargement of the radii and the formation of additional squares through divisions of the tangent points and diagonals, shown here. Mistakes are corrected with an etching knife or razor blade and not with opaque paint.

The irregularity of the tangent circles on the base grid is more striking here than in the above example. Despite extremely exact sketching, mistakes can occur from a slight shift of the compass point, the condition of the drawing board (hard- or soft-grain), or irregular ink flow, which dries at a different rate in areas in which the circles overlap.

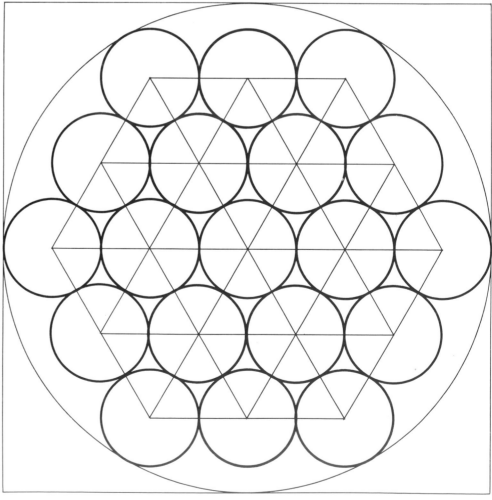

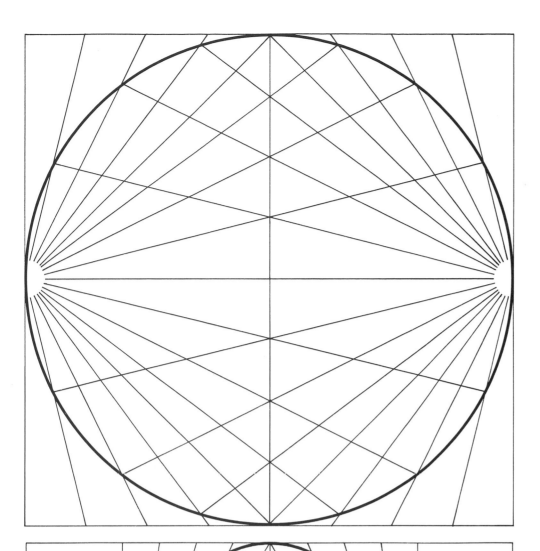

In the circle the secant and chord lines, at right angles to one another in relation to the square, are drawn regularly and symmetrically, with Thales' theorem offered as an explanation. As a variation of this exercise, a circle can be simulated by extending the fine subdivisions of the construction. If many lines converge at one point, irregular ink flow can be avoided by inserting a blank circular form.

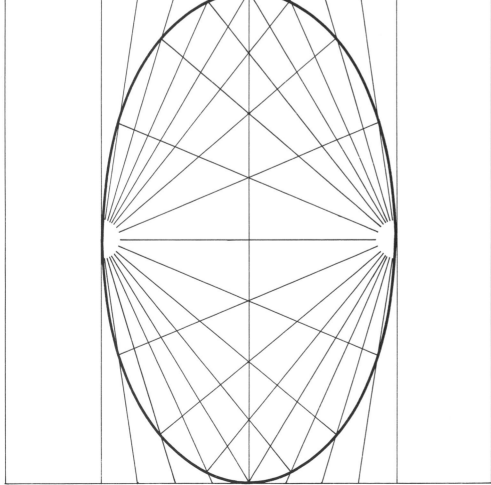

An ellipse is produced in the above construction by making proportional subdivisions of the rectangle and the symmetrical axes. Various elliptical constructions are explained. Experiments with French curves are done directly in ink on sketch paper because they require a great deal of practice.

In the isometric (one-dimensional) and diametric (two-dimensional) methods of parallel projection the representation is constructed by combining foreshortened ground and side views with the unforeshortened vertical view. This systematic method of finding spatial points is useful for the more complicated central projection.

On the right is a drawing of an axial cross in a cube. The exactness of the square touching the sides of the cube can be tested by inserting diagonals.

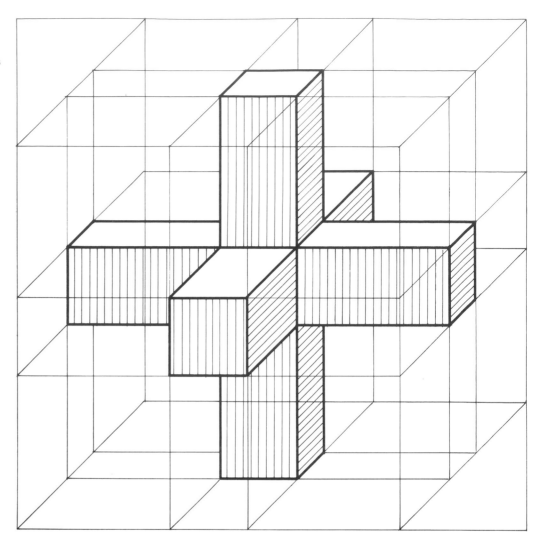

The teacher and the students are at work in the classroom.
The three photographs on the right show the correct handling of the pencil and the ruling pen.

48

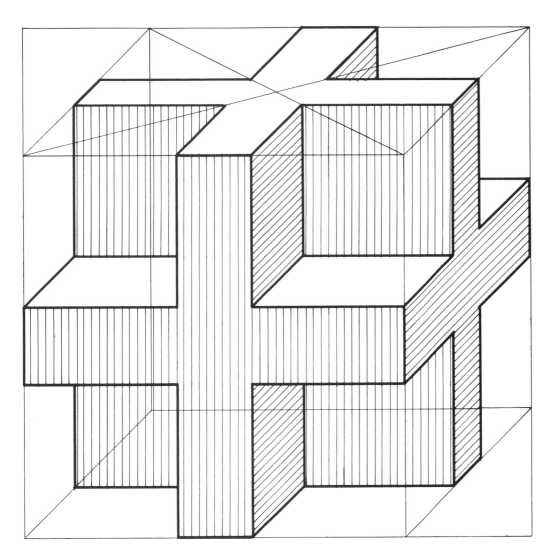

This dimensional cross is extended to the walls dividing the cube. The proportion of the frontal to the foreshortened side of the cube in the standard diametric method is 1 : 0.5. The linear grid emphasizes the overlapping surfaces. Time-consuming, difficult shadow constructions are avoided at this stage.

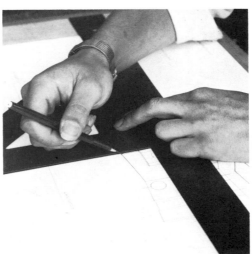

Gradated revolving prisms are sketched in relation to the base grid or to the diagonals of the square, and the ground plan is drawn precisely. In the illustration on the right the grid is drawn at the sides of the cube, enclosing the steps from which the corresponding spatial points are produced with three-part projection. The vertical, linear grid can be drawn in different densities to correspond to the angle of each level.

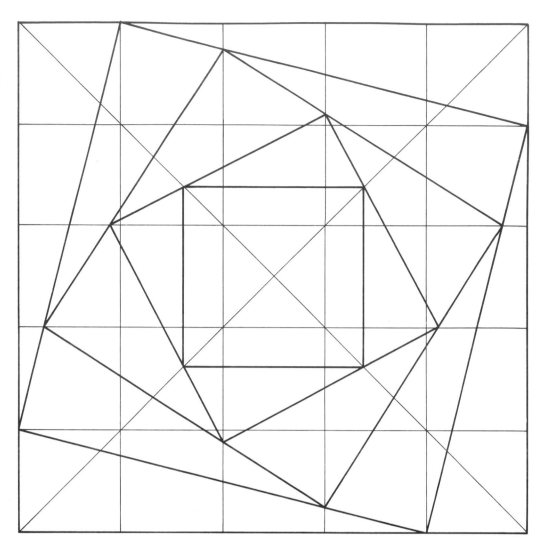

Six variations of two intersecting or penetrating cubes can be drawn with the same exterior contour and varying interior lines, producing optical illusions: the dimensions of the views from above and below are indefinite. Such figures can always be realized dimensionally and are incorrectly labeled as impossible figures.

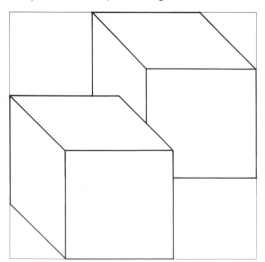 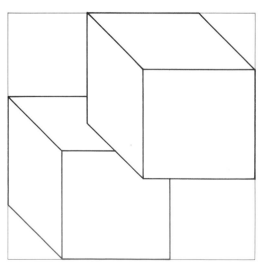 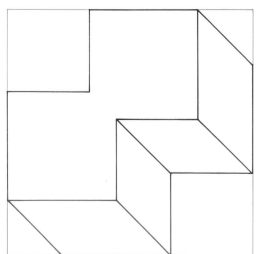

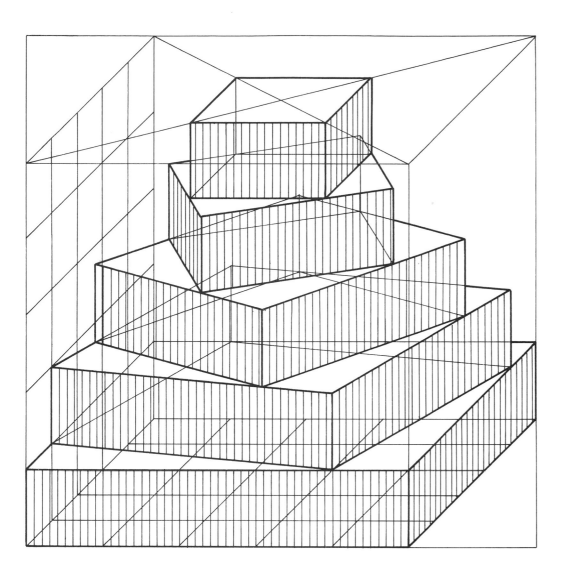

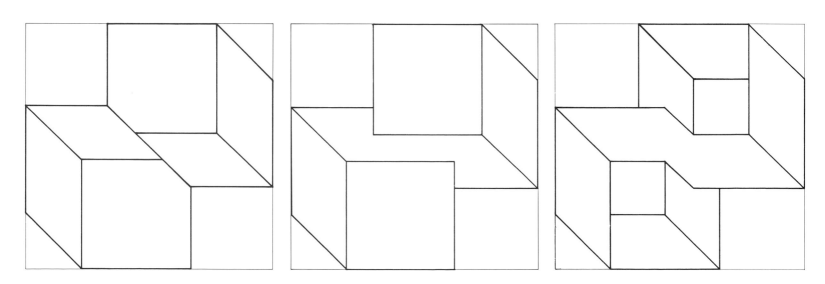

In comparison to central projection, parallel projection always appears to be slightly distorted. The clarity of the direct measurements in the drawing compensates for the disadvantageous presentation.

Simple proportion numbers replace the usual edge angles, 7° and 42° respectively, on the circumscribed square for the elevation of the cube sides. In a variation of the previously mentioned Thales circle construction the ellipses are inserted on the three visible sides of the cube.

The ellipse and cube axe in the above illustration become identical by shifting the visible outer ellipse parallel to the center of the cube. A tangential curve, cut by the three ellipses at their contours, would give the parallel projection of a sphere, an ellipsoid of rotation whose center coincides with the gravitational center of the cube.

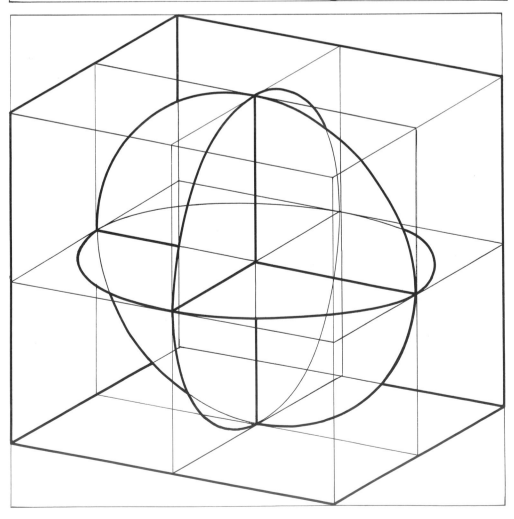

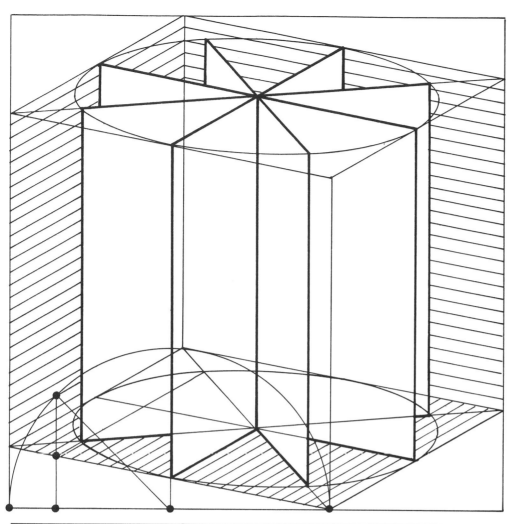

A foreshortened circle is divided into eight sections. The proportions of the angles from the half or quarter circle on the ground line are extended upward at the edge of the cube. The circle and the back corner of the cube happen to intersect in this drawing. Optional angles from the frontal circle can be transferred to the ellipse if the height proportions of the circle are inserted on the left edge of the cube.

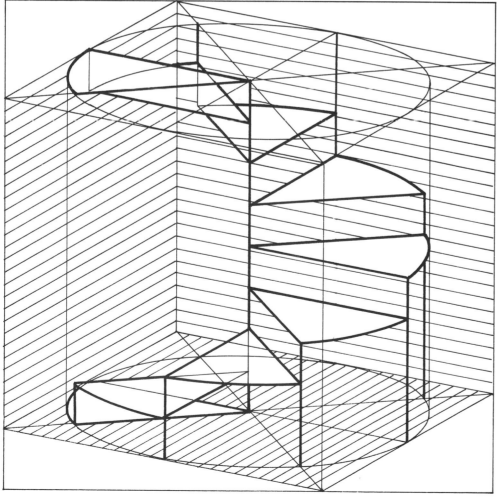

If an element is elevated and turned uniformly on an axis, it produces a screwlike or winding line that is often incorrectly called a spiral. The constructed ground ellipse with its subdivisions is shifted in a parallel direction corresponding to the individual height levels. Elevation of the ground subdivision produces the individual sectors. The enclosed cylinder forms the shaft of the resulting winding stairs.

Right-angle parallel projection of three planes is the basis of all technical drawing. It is best demonstrated with an open cube or a dimensional corner so that students can determine the form of the object. The procedure can be reversed: from two given projections of the same object the third must be found.

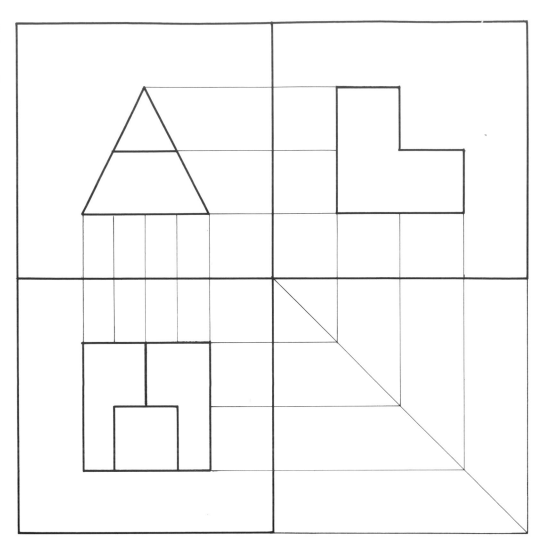

These photographs of a model with movable planes demonstrate three-part projection. The shapes and dimensional features of the model can be prepared with wires. The turned position in front of a vertical glass plate is used to explain central projection: the appropriate threads are drawn through previously determined penetration points in the glass plate to produce the perspective picture.

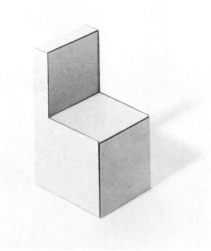
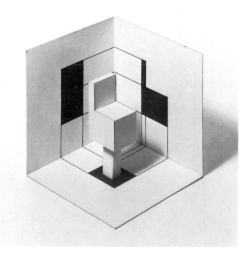
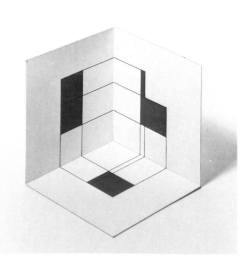

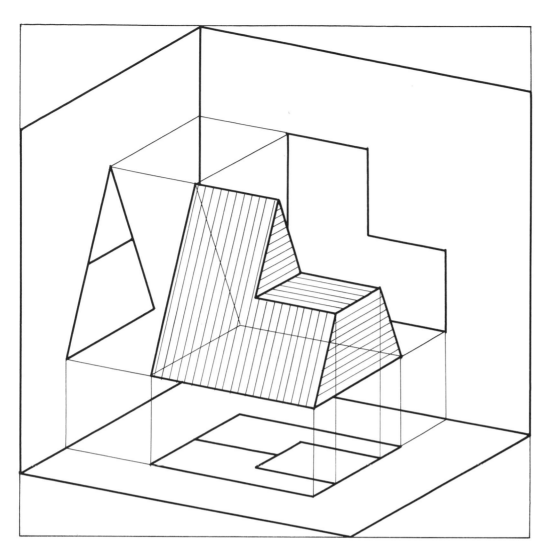

The projection planes are opened in a flat position to show the most important contours and internal lines of the object: front, ground, and side planes and front, top, and side views. A true technical drawing utilizes size, scale, material, working and tolerance specifications, cross section, and details to produce the object precisely.

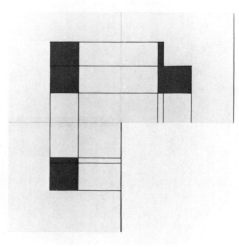

Ground and side planes of an intersecting square and a hexagonal prism are given. In the desired frontal view representation the penetration points are constructed through parallel shifting of the width and height, foreshortening individual lines at the intersection. Likewise, the entire exterior surface of such objects can be drawn on thin cardboard, cut out, and constructed as a model.

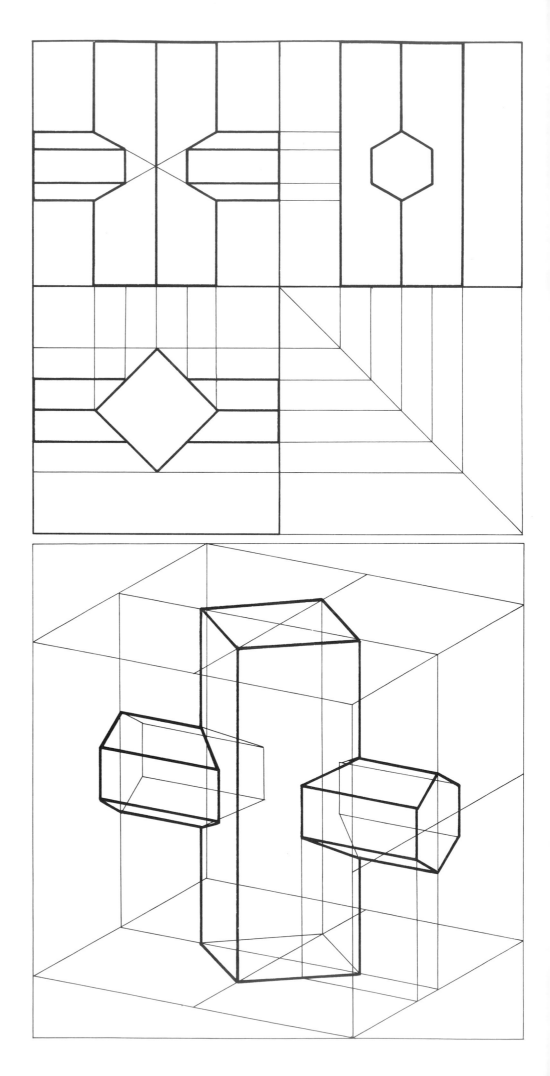

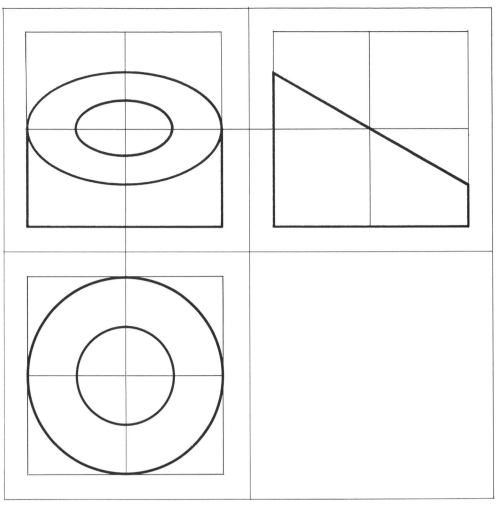

The cylinder, cut at an oblique angle to the axis of rotation, has an elliptical outline on the sectional plane. Dividing the ground-plane angles equally, transferring the ground to the side plane, and combining both views give the points of the ellipse on the frontal plane.
The students try to find further possibilities of penetrations. Difficult combinations such as cone-sphere or ring-pyramid are avoided at this stage.

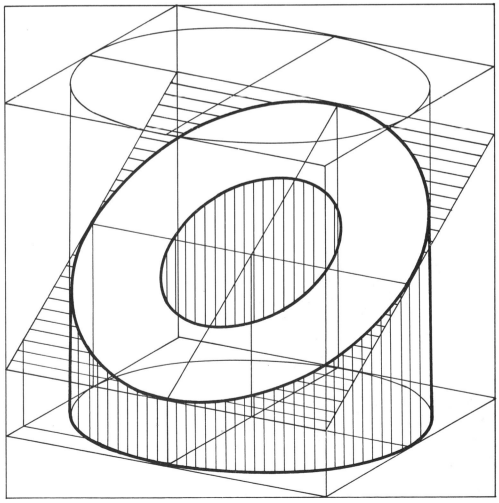

If a model of the cut cylinder is produced, it is important to determine the actual size of the sectional plane. The corresponding measurements are transferred from the ground plane at right angles to the intersecting line formed through the large axis of the ellipse. The actual lengths of the foreshortened lines are drawn on the blackboard.

Central perspective is derived empirically: it is not proven mathematically. In linear drawing objects represented in central perspective appear as if they were seen with one eye from a given viewpoint. Light rays that reach the eye from the object are replaced by constructed visual rays that strike the object from the eye. The fundamental principle of central perspective is the central projection: the visual rays of the observer penetrate an imaginary picture plane, and the penetration points produce the central-perspective image.

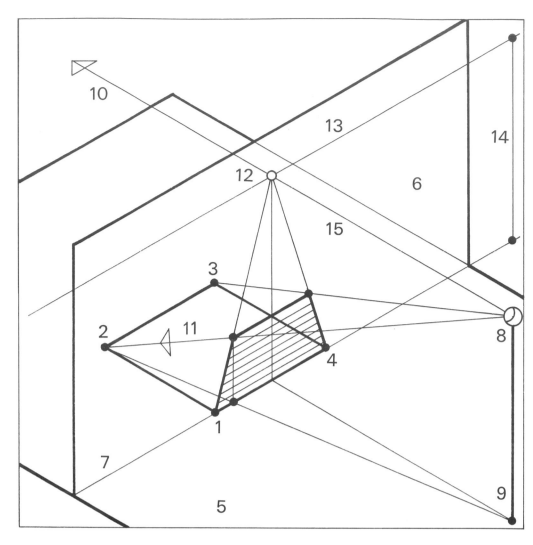

The theory is explained on the blackboard. These photographs show how the diagonal point in the model is determined and, on the right, the final perspective.

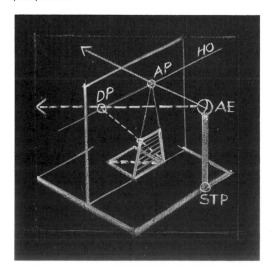

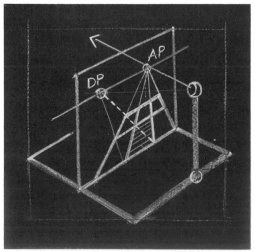

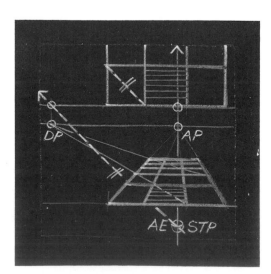

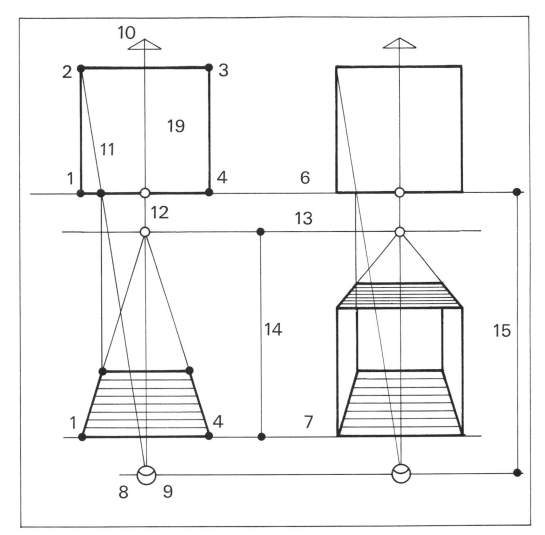

The procedure is explained with a model and represented graphically. The construction of the model exhibits the principles that the eye point is the vanishing point for all parallel lines that are perpendicular to the main visual ray and that lines parallel to the picture plane remain parallel in the projection.

Key to the numbers in the examples shown here and on the following pages:

1. corner of a square
2. corner of a square
3. corner of a square
4. corner of a square
5. ground surface
6. picture plane
7. ground line
8. eye
9. standing position
10. main visual ray
11. visual ray
12. eye point (main point)
13. horizon
14. height of horizon
15. distance
16. diagonal point
17. left vanishing point
18. right vanishing point
19. plane
20. frontal plane

If a diagonal is drawn through a unit of area (rectangular solid, cube) on the ground plane, the remaining diagonals are parallel to it and retain the diagonal vanishing point (16) through the intersection of a visual ray running parallel to the diagonal. In this way entire spaces can be constructed from a single given unit of area.

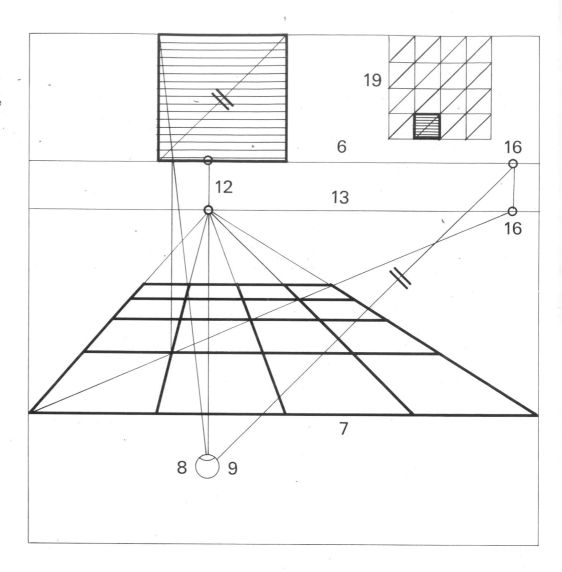

Some variations of frontal views with a cubistic space are shown from left to right: high horizon, strong floor view; normal view, extreme angles avoided; lower horizon, strong ceiling view; strong side view, spatial distortion; normal view, slightly asymmetrical: and above, in the last example the representations are rectified by twisting the object or picture plane, shown below, strong views from above and below are corrected with converging lines. This procedure is reversed in photography.

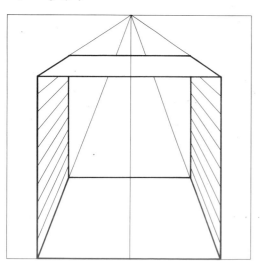
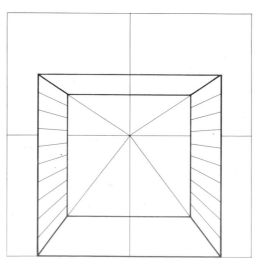
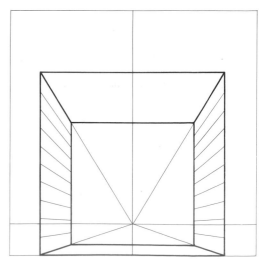

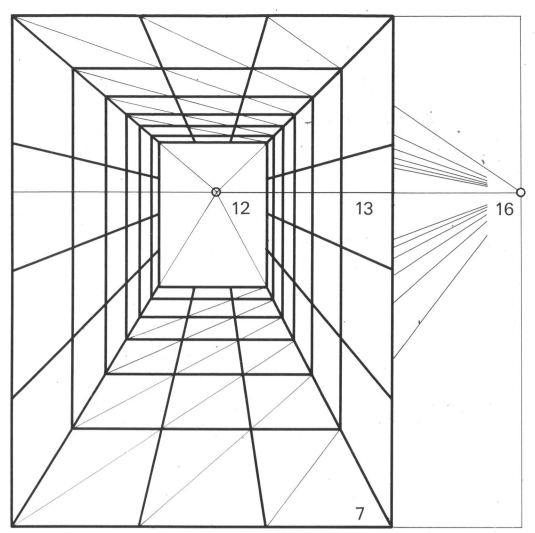

The horizon of the resulting dimensional grid is relative: the picture can be turned to change the space and the expression. If additional space is constructed beyond the ground line, the individual fields become increasingly distorted (7), similar in effect to a photograph taken with a wide-angle lens. New points can be inserted between (12) and (16) by dividing the line: halving or quartering, for example, skips of two or four units of volume, respectively, in the perspective.

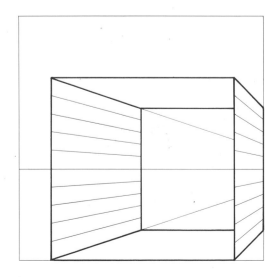

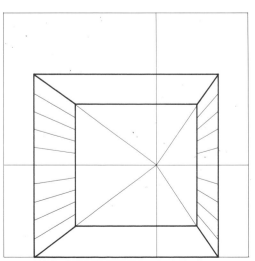

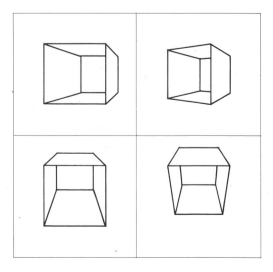

Frontal and ground planes are covered with a grid. In a reduced-ground-plane situation vanishing points are inserted and correspondingly transferred to the measurements of the enlargement at the horizon. Correct transfer of scale is possible only on the ground line and on the tangential perpendicular standing lines (measuring edges). The horizon is adjusted to the height of the space and should not coincide with the edges of objects, as in the frame on the left wall in the drawing below.

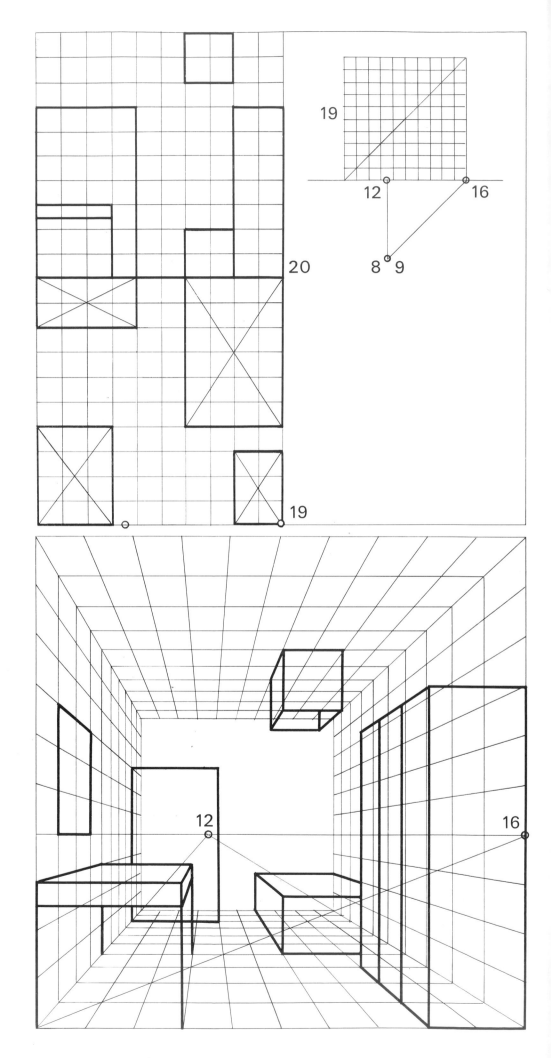

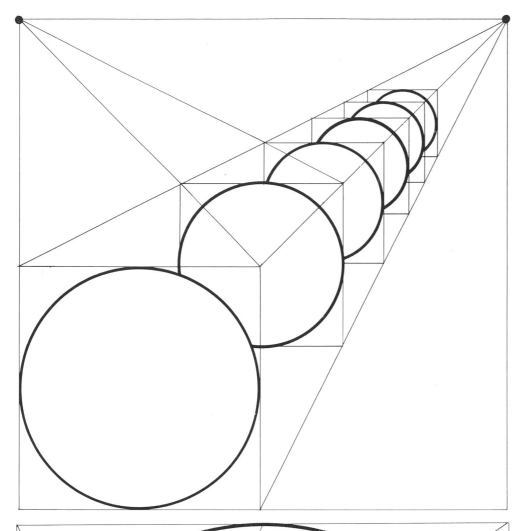

In this frontal diagram of a circle the visual rays from the points of the circle form a cone that is cut by the picture plane. The conic-section circle, ellipse, parabola, or hyperbola is produced, depending on the position of the picture plane. The circle is represented as a circle only if the axis of the cone is cut by the picture plane at a right angle. The sphere forms a circle only if its center lies on the main visual ray.

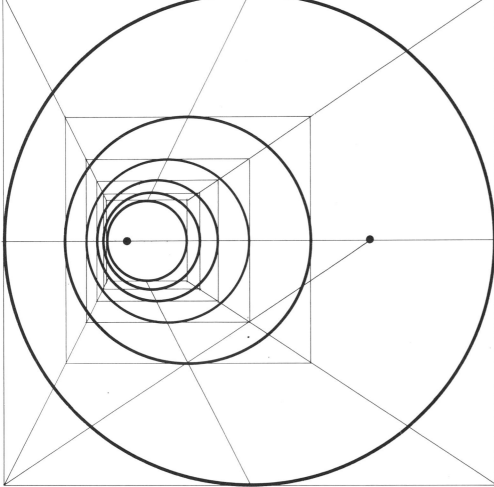

Frontal circles without overlapping shapes are foreshortened regularly in depth according to the diagonal-point principle. Such depth illusions can be further strengthened by increasing or decreasing line thicknesses, producing concave or convex effects. In the examples on the left the view looking into a tube (the largest, heaviest circle) can be changed into a view of a truncated cone (the smallest, heaviest circle).

In contrast to the preceding illustration, the object lies obliquely to the picture plane in an over-the-corner representation. Both possibilities are central perspective. The left vanishing point (17) is found with the visual ray (3) that cuts through the picture plane parallel to the sides of the square (1, 2). The right vanishing point (18) is constructed in an analogous way. The height of the object is transferred proportionally to the edges (measuring edges), tangentially to the picture plane. The object is turned at the picture plane 30°–60° corresponding to the normal drawing triangle. If a lateral vanishing point lies outside the drawing paper, the perspective depth can be found with the other lateral point and with the eye point by constructing dimensional triangles.

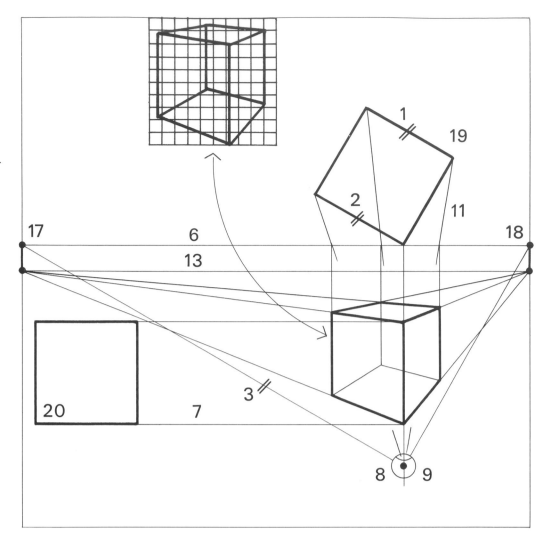

A fan structure of vanishing lines can be found by connecting the plotted proportional scales at the measuring edges and the remaining verticals. A dimensional grid can be found by inserting diagonals. Sections at the verticals can be located with the similarity ratio. The diagrams show the formation of stairs with angular or cubic steps.

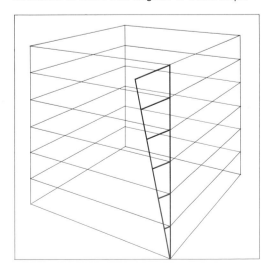
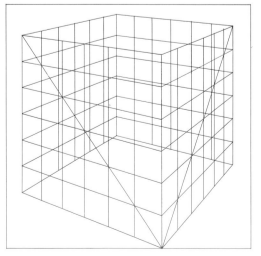
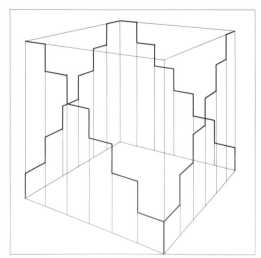

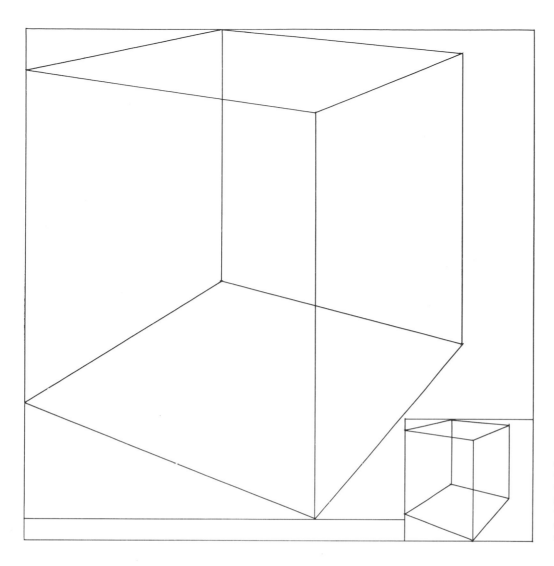

A dimensionally represented basic element (cube) can be proportionally enlarged with a grid. The enlarged illustration on the left serves as the foundation for the examples below and on the next two pages. They show how enlarged drawings can be subdivided in perspective without the use of vanishing points.

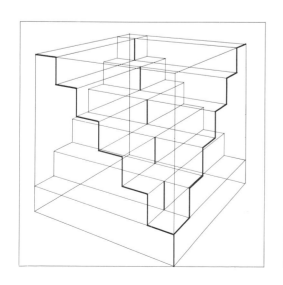

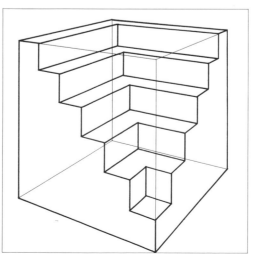

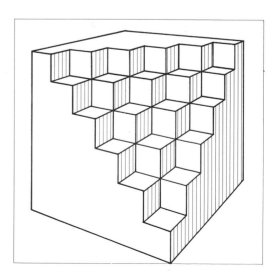

Regular perspective sections on the surfaces can be found from the sectional ground plane of the figure with visual rays or from the ground line with sectional or measuring points. The vertical subdivision on the right is constructed with regular transfers at the measuring edge and with the intersection of internal lines with diagonals.

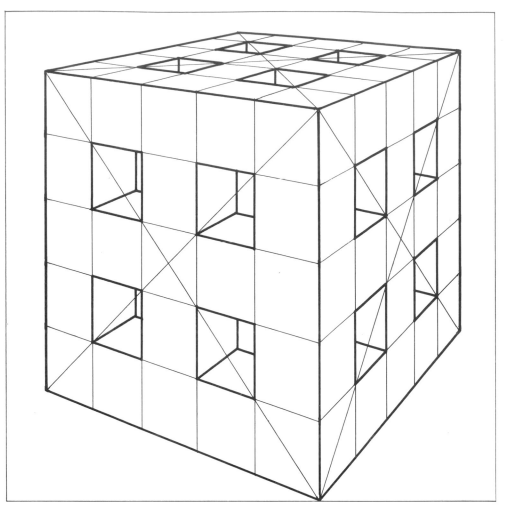

This illustration, constructed from the same grid, is an extension of the first dimensional representation (axial cross, dimensional knots). A model is likewise produced by the students. The four hollow cube knots are built from thirty-six solid cubes; the thirteen undrawn symmetrical axes and the nine symmetrical planes in each of the cubes can theoretically be extended through the entire model.

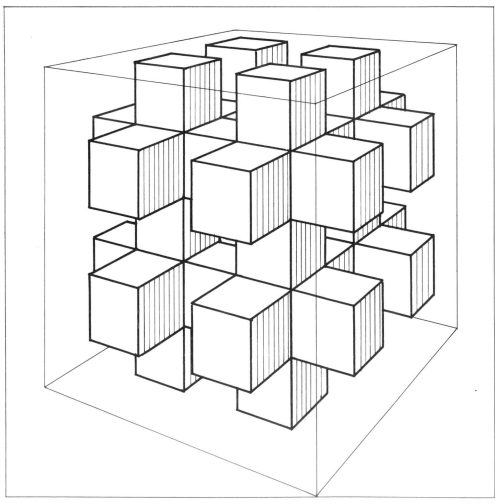

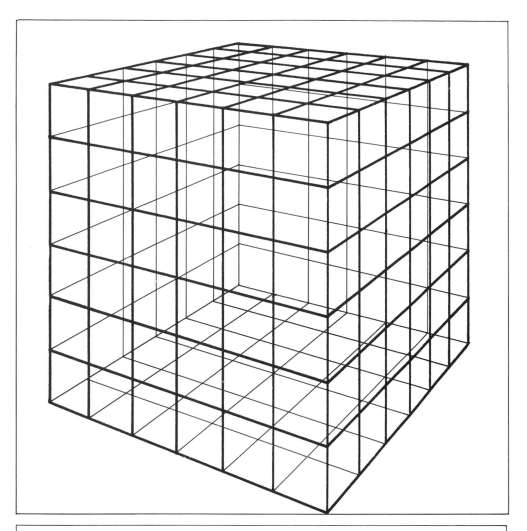

The students can trace prefabricated dimensional grids on transparent paper. Complicated dimensional details are clarified with different line weights, surface cross hatching, and colored pencils.

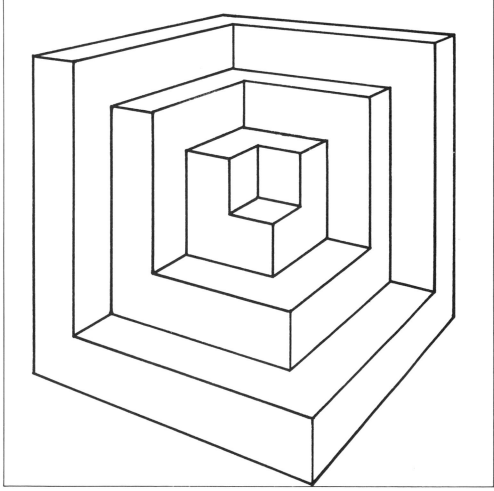

A visual inversion, a reversal from a convex to a concave illusion, can occur if you concentrate on this illustration of spatial corners. This effect would be significantly stronger in a parallel representation.

An over-the-corner representation of a ground plane turned at a 45° angle is shown here. The intersection of the object and the picture plane is different in this situation. The protruding sections are projected backwards on the plane, and the remaining penetrating points are drawn vertically downwards. Turning at equal angles to the picture plane, the deep diagonals have their vanishing point at eye point, while the frontal diagonals remain horizontal.

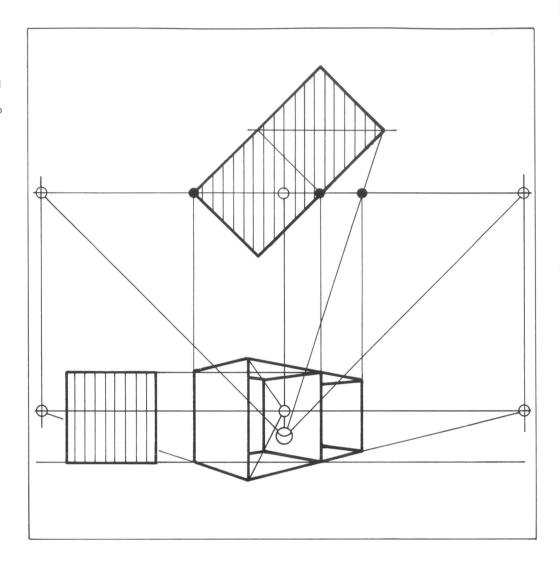

The drawings are compared with photography (central projection) to see the relationship. The photographs below left were taken with tele-photo, normal, and wide-angle lenses. Converging lines were corrected. The photographs on the right were taken with a normal lens at the same distance from the object and with different horizon heights. Converging lines (three-point perspective) were not corrected.

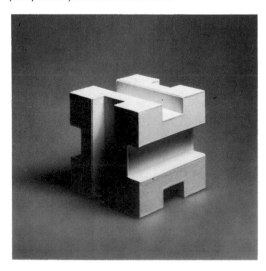
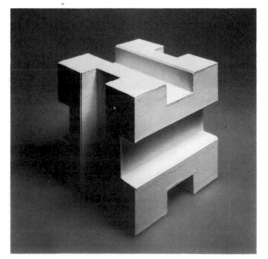

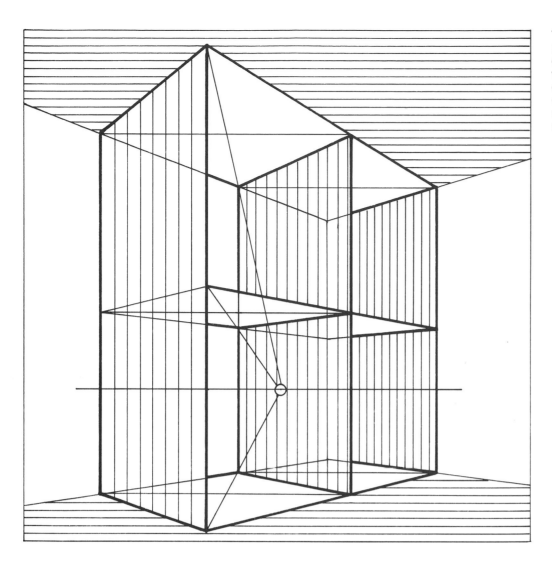

The perspective from the preceding illustration is enlarged with a linear grid. The volumetric grid can be enlarged on all sides by inserting more volumetric units and additional diagonals. Fine divisions can be added, such as tetrahedrons, octahedrons, and icosahedrons, which are mutually limited through congruent, regular polygons.

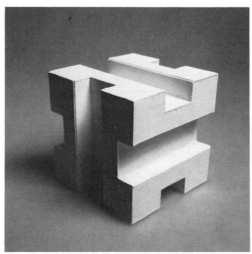
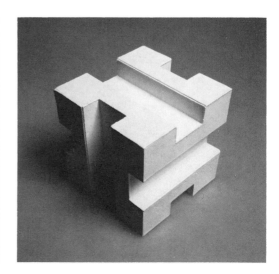

As with the frontal representation, the circle is represented as a circle only if the axis of the visible cone is perpendicular to the picture plane. The ellipse is the most common circular cross section. In the drawing the diagonal points are arbitrarily used to construct the circumscribed perspective square. Only a quarter of a circle is necessary to draw the proportions of the angles to the ground plane and to the eye point.

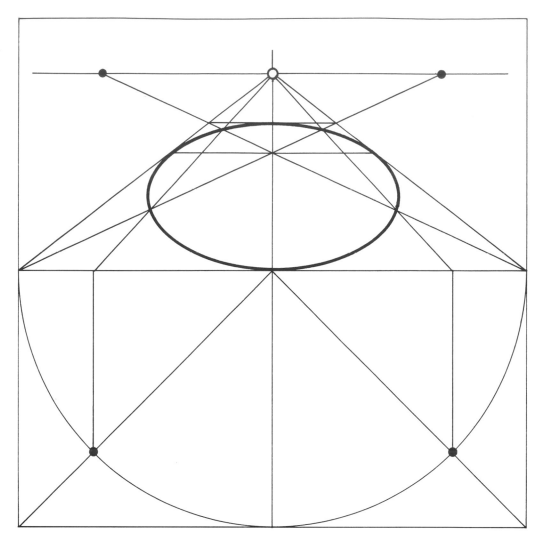

The six illustrations below show, from left to right, two examples of regular change of distance, as compared to the photographs on the two preceding pages; distortion of cubes that lie outside the human cone of vision (50° angle); the same situation with vertical distortions. In the two preceding examples the same cube is supplemented with additional cubes in depth. The enlarged illustration shows circles of vision corresponding to the angle of vision, 50° and 75°, respectively. Only the upper right part lies in the normal field of vision.

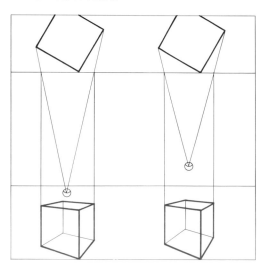

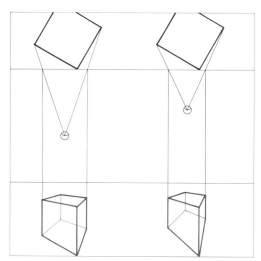

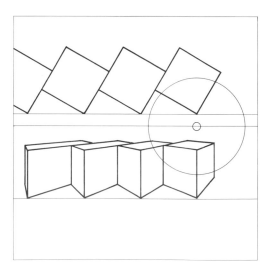

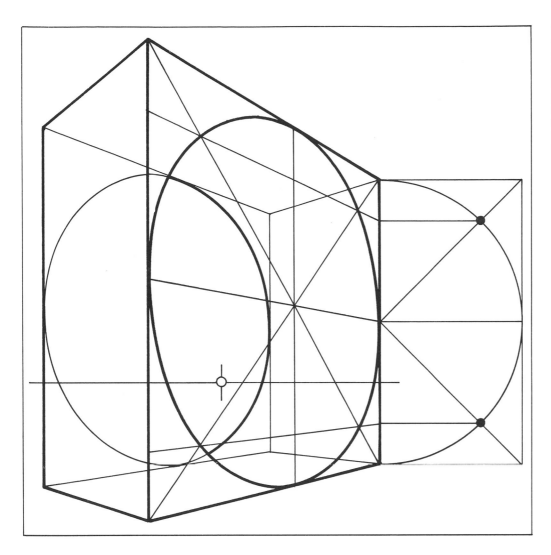

The diagonals produce the perspective center in the ellipse and the four tangent points. The largest diameter of the ellipse would be formed by inserting tangential rays of vision on the circle in the ground plane. The four additional tangent points through both ellipse axes simplify the construction of the curve. In the over-the-corner representation the frontal circle can be drawn at every optional vertical, because the proportions of the angles remain the same.

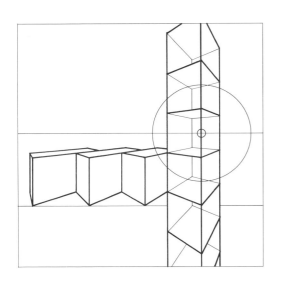

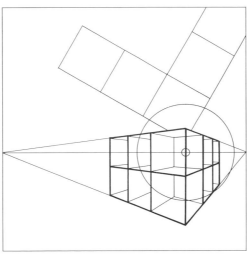

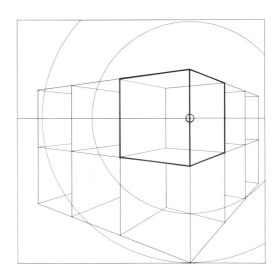

In this penetration the axes of the cylinder and half cylinder intersect at right angles. The solved perspective problem from the geometric representation, which is normally drawn in one- or two-part projection, is clearer to the observer. The curve of the intersection, the border line of the saddle surface, is found by inserting a perspective ground plane. The angle points of the cylinder drawn to the ground surface are projected to the standing surface of the half cylinder and extended up to the intersection with the convex surface lines.

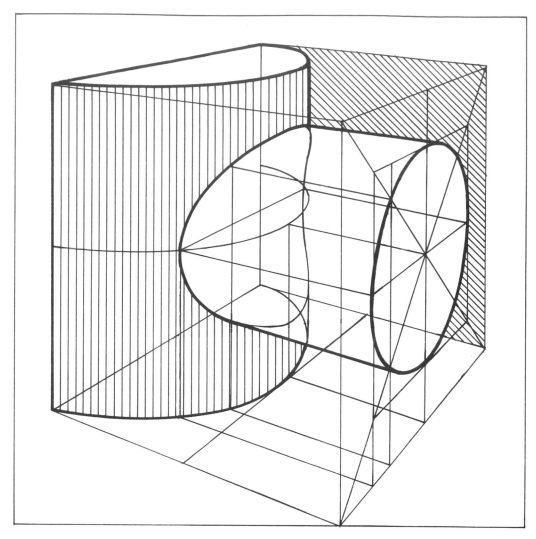

The six drawings on the blackboard show an oblique pyramid, a complementary cube, three-plane projection, the determination of the actual size from the straight lines, and the removal of both convex surfaces. The entire process is more understandable to students if they prepare a model of the object or insert straight lines and planes in an existing linear cube.

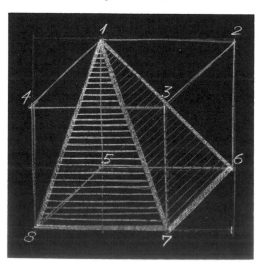
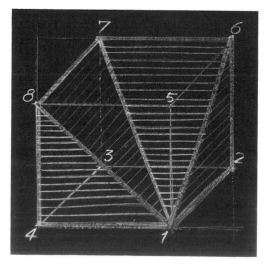
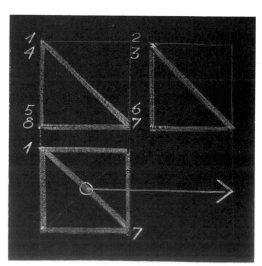

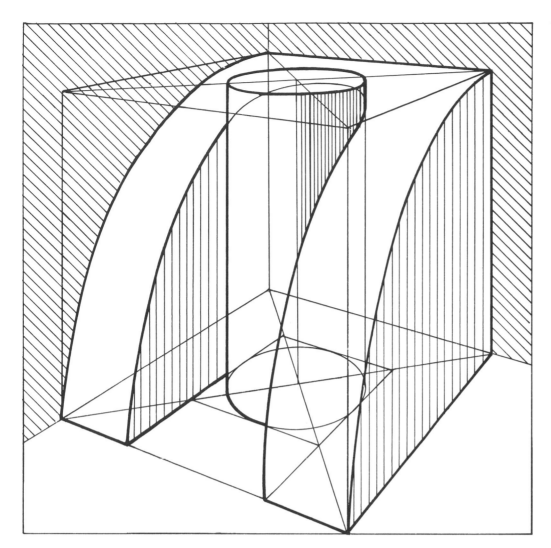

The cylinder is enclosed with a quarter circle-cube. It lies in the same over-the-corner representation as in the preceding drawing. Each quarter ellipse has another axial relationship and would approach a more circular form by extending the construction to the left vanishing point (without theoretically reaching it). The enclosing curve is seen as a half ellipse (circle) at the base and as a broken axial ellipse at the top.

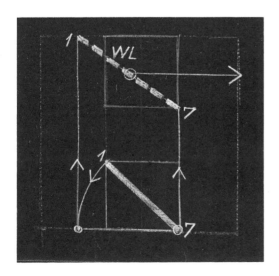
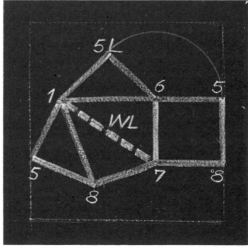
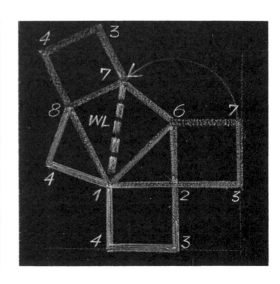

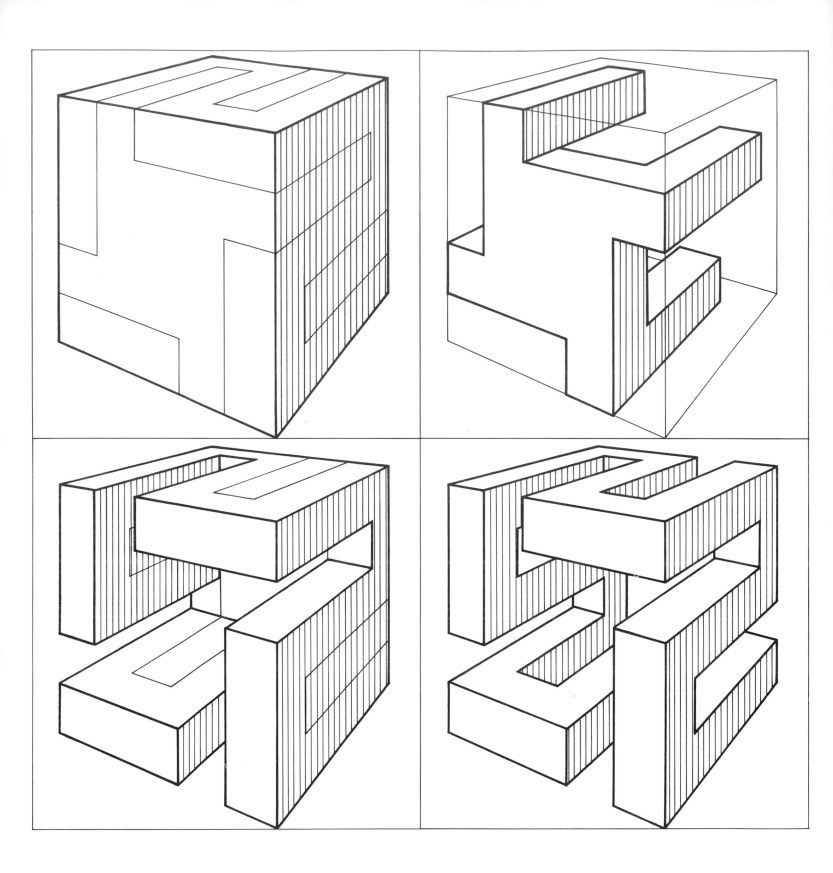

The perspective of the over-the-corner dimensional grid is taken from a previously drawn model. The illustration shows a spatial meander that forms the original cube from two identical insertable forms. More complicated combinations are produced by connecting spatial diagonals.

Lettering is the visualization of linguistic sounds by means of graphic symbols. The symbols have changed often during the course of civilization: their function as part of a graphic-communication system, their readability, and their aesthetic form are creative problems. The optical problem of readability involves the interdependence of the individual symbols and the harmonious sequence of the letters in a text, which together form the foundation of letterform education.

Graphic formulation, rhythm, and composition are achieved through systematically structured, elementary exercises using letterforms on a given writing surface. They demand concentration and manual discipline. Through constant exercise the students become aware of the formal and technical abilities required to solve complex letter problems. The appearance and formal unity of letterforms are determined by the interrelationships among basic forms of individual characters and spaces between characters and by the continuous, rhythmic properties of the strokes and the writing materials. Different exercises explore pencil, charcoal, and pen-and-ink on unruled paper. The course is organized in terms of the following interrelated disciplines: stroke and character composition, from individual strokes to nonletter symbols; elementary capital letters; and curved elements, which should exhibit the same characteristic form and correspond to fixed proportions.

The exercises are expanded by changing the writing tool from pencil to pen. Different angle positions of the pen produced variations in the relationship between vertical and horizontal strokes. Bold sketching of individual characters is encouraged. Forms and properties of letters are developed through continual redrawing. The ability to write minuscule letters results from gained knowledge. Lettering is not simply copying historical patterns or even creating beautiful calligraphy.

In addition to the practical exercises lectures are given on the present aspects and historical development of the Latin alphabet. The students also receive an insight into other writing systems.

Forming the strokes and arranging them evenly form the basis of the lettering exercises. The stroke, both an independent form and part of a letterform character, must be lively and exciting. Accentuating the ends makes its form more distinct. The accent is produced by means of stronger pressure on the writing instrument. Abrupt increases or decreases of pressure should be avoided. Pressure and counterpressure must flow homogeneously into one another. A formal unity of word and line structure and a rhythmically balanced organization of the entire page are produced through the optical equality of interior and exterior spaces between characters and line intervals. The basic interval between two verticals is the starting point of the optical adjustment. The interval is somewhat smaller than a square. Additional spaces produced with diagonals or half verticals must be optically equal to the basic interval. Individual lines are written freely on the page, which makes the optical-organization process more direct, intensive, and intuitive. It should not be influenced by helping lines.

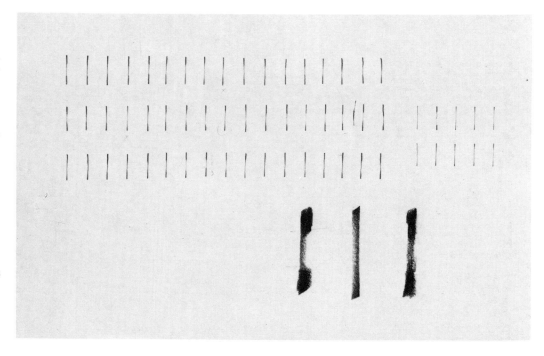

The exercises are written consecutively from left to right. The pencil must not be too soft: immediate wear produces a broad, awkward stroke. A hard pencil, on the other hand, impedes clear modulation and straightness of the stroke. The paper should not have a coarse texture, or the line will dissolve and lose its consistency. Corrections are made without erasing, and the exercise is repeated. In this way the student can compare and control the form.

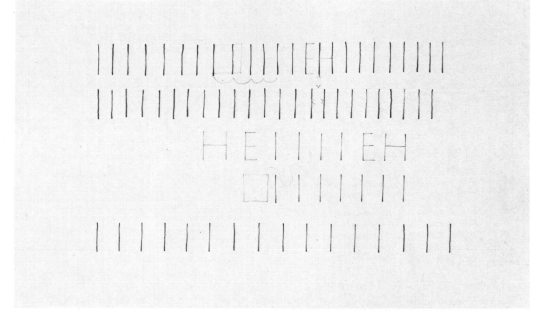

The small illustrations here and on the following pages show different problem situations and appropriate explanations or corrections. The large illustrations document the solutions.

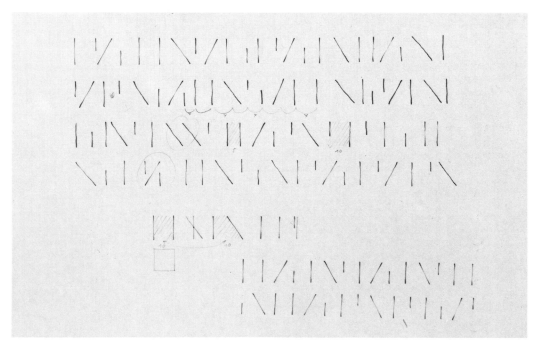

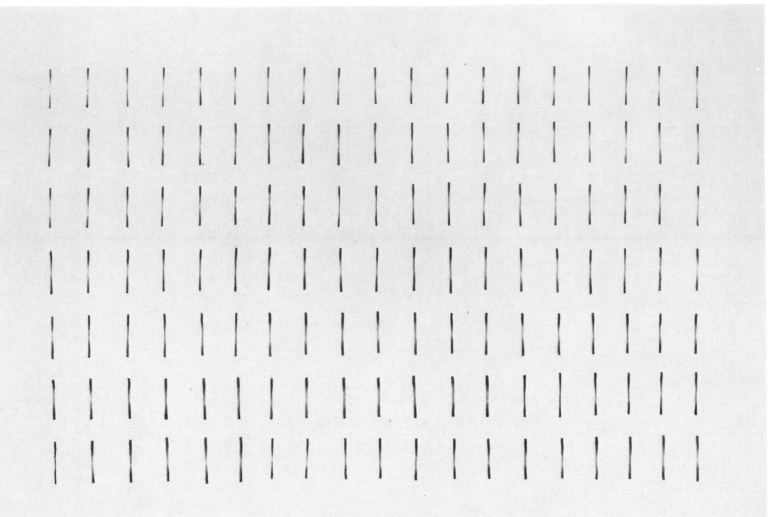

These photographs show individual writing positions. Students are not forced to use a particular hand position.

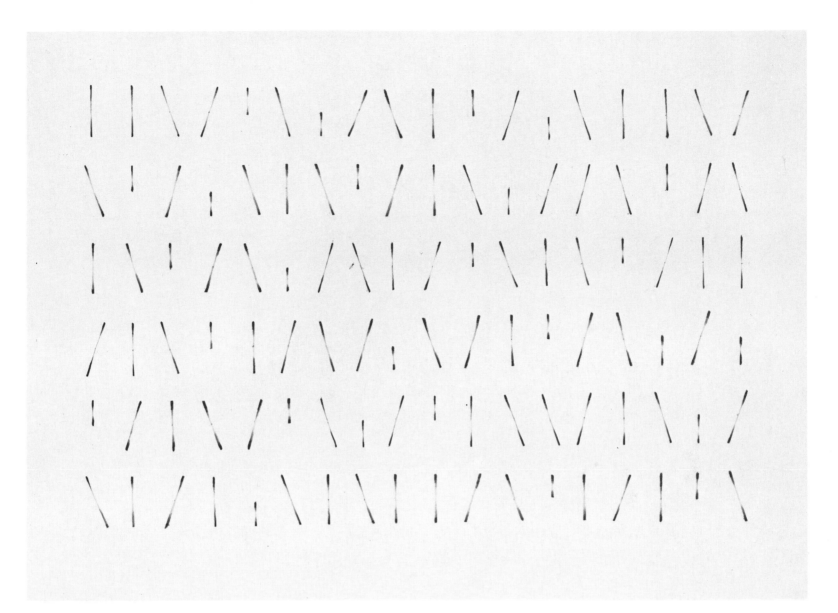

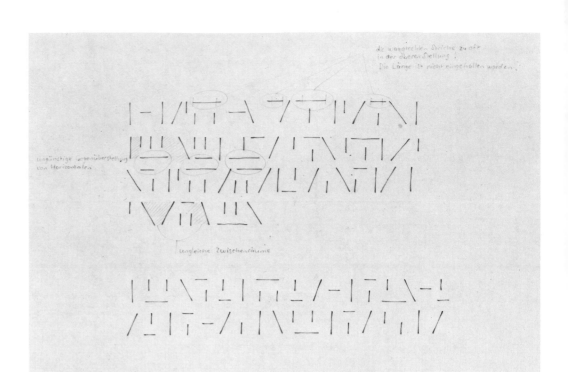

ungleiche Zwischenräume

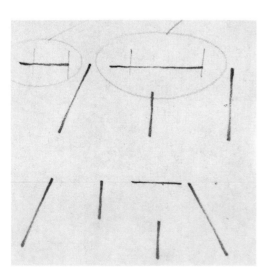

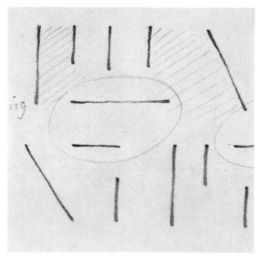

ungleiche Zwischenräume

80

The exercises include half and whole horizontal-stroke elements. In addition to stroke quality and optically equalized spacing the student must simultaneously pay attention to the uniform, quantitative distribution of given stroke elements. All the parts should form a balanced unity of quantity, organization, and rhythm.

The enlarged section from the illustration above left shows unrhythmic spacing. The spaces are optically unequal, and the standardized linear lengths vary.

The curve is the final element in the basic exercises. Its clear, definite form essentially determines the characteristics of written capitals and round letters. The curve is fundamentally symmetrical and wider than the geometric half circle. The form should end either horizontally or slightly rounded.

The enlarged sections show corrections of curve characteristics.

When the student is sure of his letter-building elements, symbols are organized into a composition. A predetermined number of elements is used. The structure of the forms should be simple: they should not contain more than three linear elements. The creative and inventive capacities of the students are stimulated through this exercise, which is a preliminary to actual letter writing. It summarizes the most important components of letter writing: technical discipline, concentration, understanding, and sensitivity to form, rhythm, and organization.

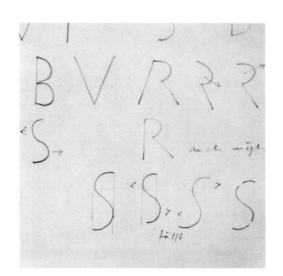

zu flach
mehr elliptisch

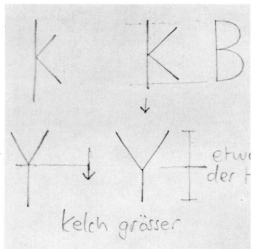

kelch grösser

ESOXCONVERSVS
ABANTONIOCVM
CONIVGEETSVO
ILIOSVRGEBATVI
RIBVSMORALIBVR
SNONVESCENS

BCDGOPQRSKXYZ
XRQKBDYPGZSOC
SYGPRZKBXODCQ
DOBCSRZQRYGXK KB
RKGXBOSDZQPCY Y

zu flach
mehr elliptisch
B P

kelch grösser

ISTVCQVIDEML
AELITNECESSES
TSEDQVONIAM
AMICITIAPERG
BORATVSGRAL
IPSECONFIDER
EMIHISACNOI

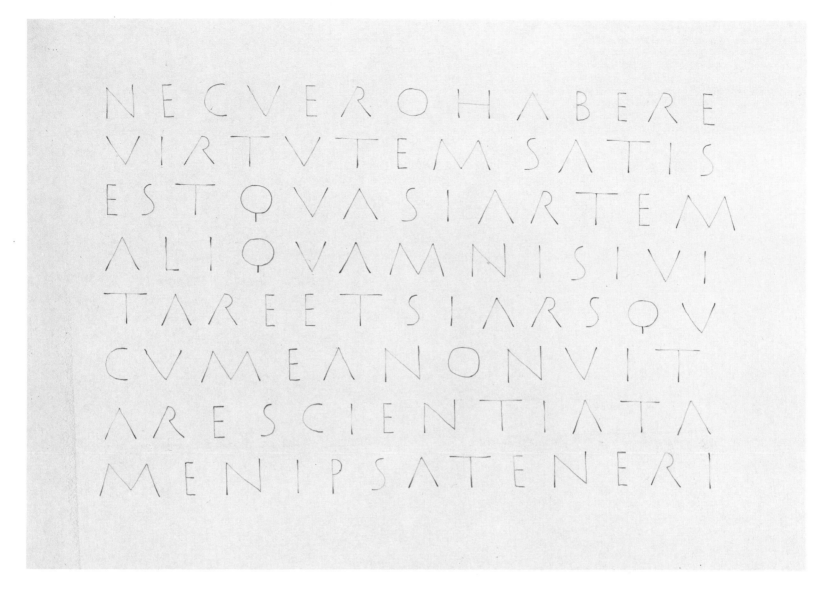

Following this necessary foundation the students concentrate on the formulation of alphabetic symbols. Transcribing a Latin text is a suitable introduction to capital letters. Intervals between words are not considered in order to concentrate on organizing the lettering surface. Experience from the preceding exercises is transferred to the letters. Proportions between and within the individual symbols must be recognized and used correctly, and the different forms must be arranged according to size and degree of openness in a clear optical relationship to the total composition: for example, the letter O is small because of its closed nature; the termination of the letter N ascends slightly to the right and is compensated for by its two pointed angles. Each student works from the same model, but personal texture is developed. Individual organization, form, and general appearance deviate slightly from one another without differing essentially from the standard model.

The enlarged sections show corrections of the forms and proportions of individual signs. The curve of the R, above right, should not be pulled down but slightly elevated. The vertical position of the S is produced by aligning the ending strokes vertically with the width of the letterform. The width of the curves in B and P, center, is very small. In the complete picture the forms appear narrow because of this incorrect proportioning. The vertical of the K, below, should be slightly longer than the normal character height. The starlike appearance of the form neutralizes its relatively long diagonals. The meeting point of the lines in the Y are just below the geometric center.

In the beginning of the exercise spontaneous, direct, correct writing of complicated letters (such as B, R, S) is difficult. In order to understand the essential characteristics of such forms, students sketch on large sheets of newsprint. Correct proportional construction and form are analyzed while practising in a free, sketching technique. The selection of writing utensils is left to the students: they can use a soft 6B pencil, brush and ink, lithographic crayon, or charcoal.

These three illustrations show examples of finished forms done in brush and ink, charcoal, and lithographic crayon.

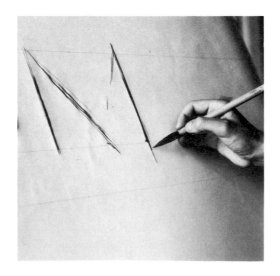

The following photographs show individual writing positions. A standing position allows a fluid, unhindered rhythm and a simultaneous observation of forms at a greater distance.

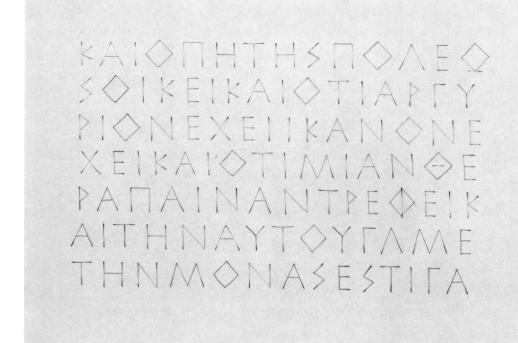

Writing a text involves clear organization and formulation of alphabetic characters within a linguistic context. The contents are initially irrelevant, so the exercise can be done with non-Latin alphabets such as Greek or Cyrillic. All of these alphabets have a similar formal basis, so the same principles can be applied.

In the lettering classroom questions and problems are discussed and explained in groups and individually.

KAIOΠHTHSΠOΛ
EΩΣOIKEIKAIOTI
APΓYPIONEXEIP
KANONEXEIKAI
OTIMIANΦEPAΠ
AINANTPEΦEIKA
ITHNAYTOYΓΛM

The lettering pen creates a completely different effect than pencil. The contrasting rhythm of thick and thin line segments within the individual letters produces a dynamic quality, and students can clearly experience the direct influence of the tool on the lettering form. The lettering pen also allows exploration of the calligraphic aspects of the Latin alphabet. The exercise is produced with a Soennecken-pen No. 2 or the English Mitchell-Roundhand No. $1^1/_2$. Black ink ist mixed equally with water to obtain a lighter line. A color relationship between the writing and the surface is produced by using absorbent, yellow-toned paper. In general, Ingre paper is suitable for writing with pen and ink.

The pen is held in a fixed position so that the writing edge of the oblique-cut point is absolutely horizontal. This allows the greatest possible line contrast. Applying pressure on the writing tool is essential to the creation of thick vertical and diagonal strokes. With pressure the line becomes thicker because of the spreadable pen nib. A uniform change of pressure modulates the stroke. The student learns the principles of structure and regularity for the Roman letter-forms, which exhibit strong contrasts of stroke thickness and modulation of individual thick strokes.

In the two above examples line modulation and letter formation, especially the S, are schematically explained.

The following photographs show the different pen positions for writing the M.

VENIONVNCADF
ORTISIMVMSVIR
VMAXIMVMIQV
ECONSILIOMNIB
ARBARORVEXCE
PTISDVOBVSCAR
THAGIENESIBVS

In comparison to the pencil exercises forming capital letters with the pen is more dependent on technical ability, writing material, and formal perception. The contrasting pen strokes are sketched on large newsprint paper in order to recognize their characteristics within the fluid structure of the letterform.

The examples here and on the following two pages show two technically different methods of sketching letterforms: sketching the contours and filling in the forms or sketching with the broad edge of the writing tool (lithographic crayon or charcoal).

Formal problems are explained at the blackboard.

The photographs below left show blackboard explanations of problems such as curve development, form width, and letter spacing. The right-hand illustration shows students sketching. The large sketching paper is fixed on a movable tabletop. An oblique or vertical working surface enables the students to observe and control the large forms from a distance.

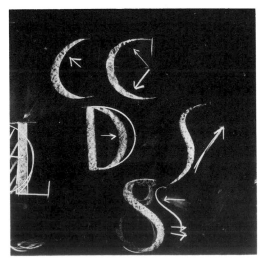

Optically adjusted placement of neutral signs and rhythmically balanced organization of the surface are also practised with the pen. Three elements—diagonal, vertical, and curve—are prerequisites for these exercises. They are combined into characters with two parts. The illustrations show two different but equally balanced compositions.

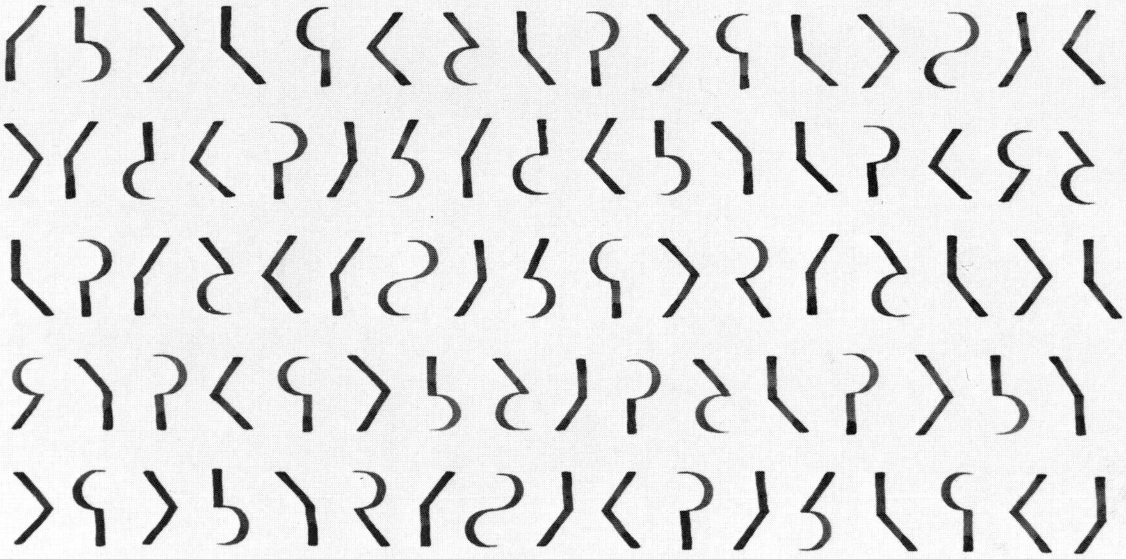

INILLOTEMPOREDIXITIHSUSDISCIPULIS
SUISPARABOLAMHANCSIMILERITRIG
NUMCAELORUMDECEMUIRGINIBUS
QUAEACCIPIENTESLAMPADESSUASEXIERR
UNTOBUIAMSPONSOETSPONSAEQUIN
QUEAUTEMEXEISERANTFATUAETQUI
INQUEPRUDENTESSEDFATUAEACCEPTIS

In the two preceding exercises the characters are written slowly. The wide metal nib does not allow quick execution of individual lines and letters, but more spontaneous strokes are possible with pencil, brush, or charcoal because they offer no resistance to the writing movement.

The illustrations show the optical and rhythmical organization of an uppercase text. Conscious control is subordinate to spontaneous, quickly executed writing movements. In this instance felt-tip pens of different hardnesses and sizes are used.

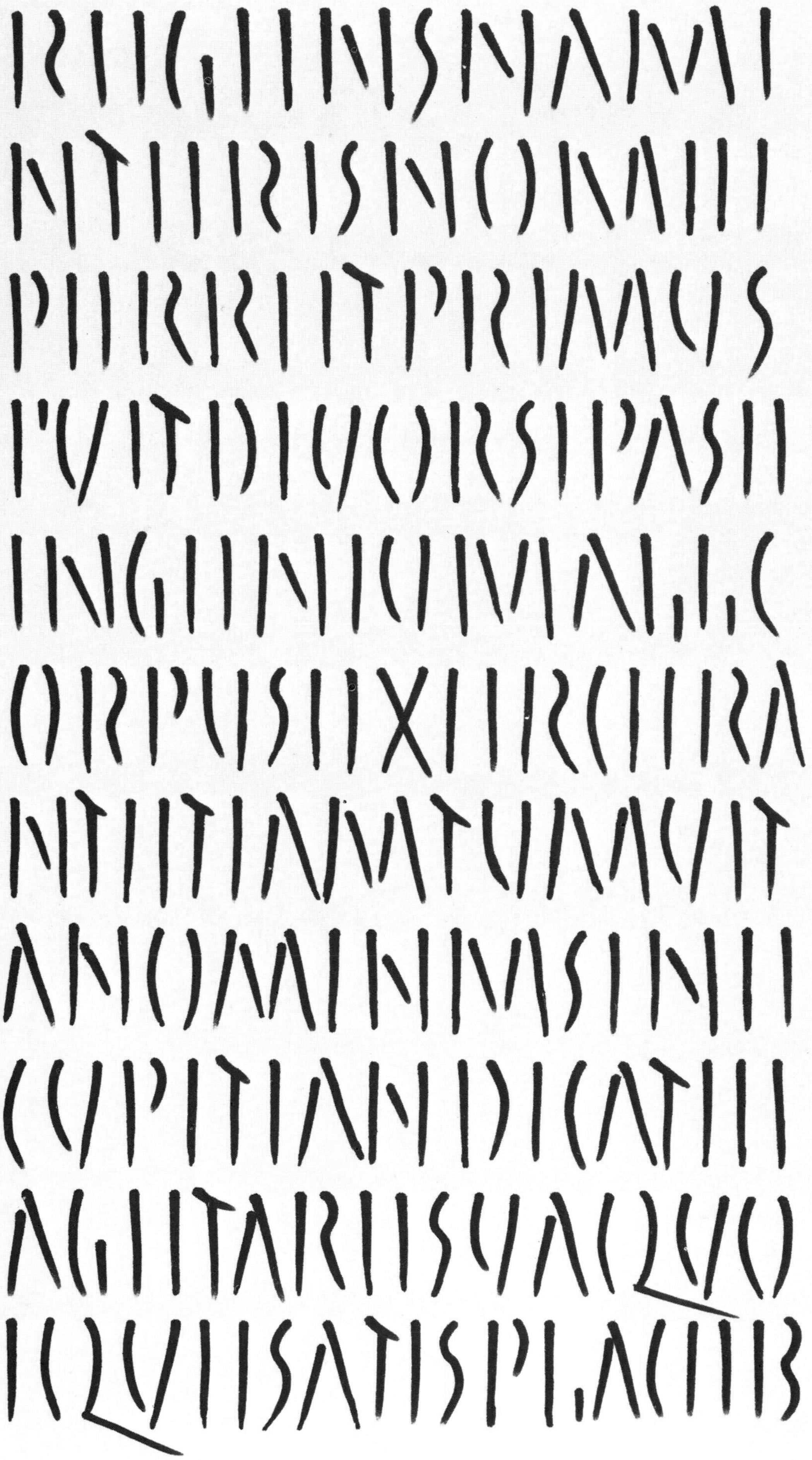

Less contrast between horizontal and vertical lines weight can be produced by changing the pen position from a horizontal to a diagonal angle. The curves shift axially from a vertical to a diagonal position. These letters appear more fluid in comparison to the preceding examples with stiff forms. As the letter structure changes with the angle of the pen, students become aware of fundamental possibilities of calligraphy.

ABCDEFGHKLMN ᄃᄃᄃ
OPRSTVXZABCDFFD
ABCDEFGHIKLMN A
OPRSTVXYZDILEY EEE
ESOXCONVERVSA
BANTONIOCVMC

These illustrations show changes in line contrast and in curves corresponding to the pen position. A 14° to 21° angle produces a contrasting relationship between horizontal and vertical lines.

PER TOTVM RRT
ΛΛΛΙ 'AA 'B PB
BBBBBB Γ B·B
B B3
IB

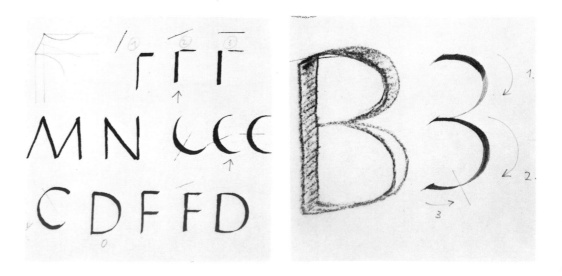

NECVEROHABEREVIRTETV
TEMSATISESTQVASIARTEM
ALIQVAMNISIVITARIETSI
ARSQVIDEMCVMEANONV
ITARESCIENTIATAMENIPS
ATENEREPOTESTVIRTVSIN
VSVSVITOTAPOSITAESTVS
VSAVTEMEIVSESTMAXIMV

MEDIAAVTEM
NOCTECLAMO
RFACTVSESTEC
CESPONSVSVE
NITEXITEOBV

Writing lowercase letters is quite different from capital letters. In contrast to the individual, unconnected forms of capital letters, lowercase letters depend on optical and calligraphic connections between the characters, organization of the text into separate words, and clear separations between the lines. The lowercase letters allow for a fluid writing text. The rhythmic uniformity of the writing movements produces a personal texture. The integration of capitals into the lowercase text and the correct proportions of ascenders and descenders to the x-height are essential components in this exercise.

These illustrations show the students' initial difficulties in clarity, fluidity, and rhythm. The large illustration on the right shows a lowercase text without word spacing or capital letters. Uniform spacing between the characters is stressed. The illustration on the last page shows an organized text with cursive, lowercase letters.

The photographs on the right-hand page show sections from blackboard explanations. The beginning and end of the vertical line are strengthened through pressure. In straight-standing and cursive lowercase letters—for example—the traditional connection begins at the bottom of the stem. The head of the t is just above the line of the body height, and the f curve should not extend too far to the right.

iurisutriusquedoctoremin
universitateromanaprofesso
rememeritumquiincompar
abiliususnonsolumiurissed
palaeographinequoqueets
archaeologiaescientiapluri
mauirisantiquisdocumenta
extitulispapyrismembranis

Wenn eine Kultur, einer der Versuche der Domestizierung des Menschen müde wird und zu wanken beginnt, dann werden die Menschen in immer grösserer Zahl merkwürdig, werden hysterisch, haben sonderbare Gelüste, gleichen jungen Leuten in der Pubertät oder Schwangeren. Es regen sich in der Seele Dränge, für die man keinen Namen hat, die man von der alten Kultur und Moral aus als schlecht bezeichnen muss, die aber mit so starker, mit so natürlicher, mit so unschuldiger Stimme sprechen können, dass alles Gute und Böse zweifelhaft wird und jedes Gesetz ins wanken kommt.